CONTENTS

"SOLD AMERICAN!"

—THE FIRST FIFTY YEARS

The American Tobacco Company

*Powhatan, symbol of American Tobacco, was a chief
of Virginia Indians. His daughter Pocahontas wed
John Rolfe, the first white man of the Jamestown
settlement to grow a commercial crop of tobacco.*

4

FOREWORD

ON OCTOBER 19, 1904, The American Tobacco Company in its present legal form came into being. In a legal sense, then, this history marks our fiftieth anniversary.

Like many other statistics, this one tells a very incomplete story. In point of time, American Tobacco goes back a good deal farther than its 1904 re-incorporation. Under a different corporate structure but with the same name, the Company goes back to 1890. And the management of The American Tobacco Company traces in an unbroken line all the way from 1865, when Washington Duke and his sons started a home tobacco manufactory in their little log cabin outside Durham, North Carolina.

In point of manufacturing tradition, American Tobacco is even older. The *Lucky Strike* brand, for instance, was begun as a smoking tobacco mixture by a subsidiary company founded in Richmond in 1853. Some of the fine Havana cigars made by the Company go back even farther.

In point of product, our enterprise has its roots in the pre-Columbus years when the misnamed "Indians" of this hemisphere grew tobacco to be smoked in crude pipes and rolled into rough cigars and cigarettes. With the passage of time and the acquisition of knowledge, tobacco and its curing and manufacture have been greatly changed, greatly refined. But the leaf seems to give the same solace to modern, civilized Americans that it yielded the naked savages of five centuries ago. This is not so strange as it may sound at first; for the cigarette holds enjoyment for many different kinds of people in our own day. A *Lucky Strike,* or a *Pall Mall,* or a *Herbert Tareyton,* can be smoked with pleasure by a farmer between furrows, a G.I. in Korea, a clerk "taking five" from his office desk, or a well-dressed patron in some fashionable dining place.

Whatever age we assign The American Tobacco Company, wherever we place the start of the American smoking tradition, we are not celebrating numbers alone. It is true that this Company has made and sold more cigarettes than any other. And it is true that its founders changed the nation's smoking tastes with their bold gambles on machinery, and on

fresh uses of the printed word. But by these tokens it is also true that our Company has had more experience in cigarette making, more opportunity to learn our business, than any other.

This means that we have managed to plow that knowledge back into our blending and testing and leaf-buying and manufacturing over the years. If we had not, if our experience were not reflected in the highest quality men and machines can attain, some other company would be the leading manufacturer of cigarettes.

We are confident that we shall remain so, that Americans will continue to use our products at an accelerating rate.

Our confidence is based on two things. First, tobacco itself has been part of the American heritage as long as men have lived in this favored corner of the world: even the cliff-dwellers of the New Mexico desert left smoking implements behind them. Second, it is American Tobacco's policy to place quality of product above all other considerations. We believe this policy accounts for our volume of business, and so make it the starting point for everything we do. We believe it is best for our customers, our employees, our stockholders, our suppliers and for the American tradition of smoking.

Unlike many a volume business, ours does not stand or fall on this year's new design or next year's fashion, for smoking tastes change slowly. We gather the best tobacco leaves we can find, age and blend and flavor and shred them. We package and pass them on to the smoker in the form he prefers, rolled in white paper or Havana leaf or Connecticut wrapper or packed in tins. But the heart of our business—the tobacco—is recognizable in any of these forms. It originated in American soil; it is sanctioned by ancient custom; it is part of our habit of life.

So we are proud to dedicate "Sold American!" to the American public. Their good taste has made it all possible.

Paul M. Hahn

Paul M. Hahn
President

The first Americans—those seen by Columbus in the West Indies—smoked burning rolls of tobacco, also sniffed it through a Y-shaped tube. The Spaniards confused tube, or tobago, with leaf. Thus, tobacco.

THE MAKINGS OF A NATION

THEY CAME for gold, and they found tobacco. The first American smoker they saw was puffing a primitive cigarette. Two of the mariners described it as a huge "firebrand": dried tobacco leaves wrapped in leaves of palm or maize.* The date was November 6, 1492, less than a month after the three ships anchored off San Salvador. Wrote Bartholomio de Las Casas, who later edited the journal of Christopher Columbus: "The natives wrap the tobacco in a certain leaf, in the manner of a musket formed of paper . . . and having lighted one end of it, by the other they suck, absorb or receive that smoke inside with their breath."

Almost four centuries went by before James B. Duke, founder of The American Tobacco Company, rediscovered the cigarette. It was not until he did that Americans took up smoking in a big way. The cigarette, as the folk of Duke's day were to discover, is tailor-made for an industrialized, urbanized, hurry-up society. It fits neatly into the chinks of respite that break up a busy day. It requires less paraphernalia than a pipe, less leisure time than a cigar, less attention than either. And it is a more universal form of tobacco consumption than "eatin'

*A cigar is a roll of smoking tobacco wrapped in a tobacco leaf. A non-tobacco wrapper makes it a cigarette.

tobacco," whose rough-and-ready appeal is almost specifically masculine.

The first Americans, however, were neither industrialized nor in a hurry. They did not require careful blending, delicate flavoring or precision wrapping in cellophane. But they did relish tobacco in some form, primitive or no. And the first explorers of the Carib islands and the South Atlantic littoral soon came to share their pleasure in the "Soverane Herbe."

With French and English vying with Spaniards for footholds in the New World, it is not surprising that the plant should have received many names. West Indian natives used a Y-shaped piece of hollow cane as a pipe for smoking or sniffing tobacco. Columbus himself is supposed to have used their word for this instrument, *tobago*, to describe a Y-shaped Caribbean island still called Tobago. The Spanish themselves preferred the weed in its rolled form; the word cigar is theirs.

The Sacred Book of the Quiché Mayans indicates smoking was an honored practise in Guatemala long before its conquest by one of Hernàn Cortès' captains. The Lords of Xibalba, goes the legend, held council by the light of fat-pine torches and smoked cigars. Tobacco was "ziq" in Quiché and the verb for

The proper name of it amongst the Indians is *Picielt*. The name For the name of *Tabeco* is giuen to it by our Spaniards, by reason of an Iland that is named *Tabaco*.

It is an hearbe that doeth growe and come to bee very great: many times too bee greater then a Lemmon tree. It casseth foorth one steame from the roote which groweth vpright, without declining to any parte, it sendeth foorth *The description of it.*

Monardes' "Newes of the New-found Worlde" in 1596 pictured leaf: "The name of Tabaco is given to it by Spaniards by reason of an Island named Tabaco."

Exploring the St. Lawrence in 1535, Jacques Cartier saw Indians carrying small bags of tobacco around their necks, but it "bit our tongues like pepper."

smoking, "zikar." Perhaps this had some relation to the Spanish "cigarro." Whatever the word's origin, Spain was quick to discover that the leaf grown in Cuba made the finest cigars.

Pipes, pikes and petum

Farther north on the mainland, where the first skirmishes of the battle for the New World were fought between Spaniards and French, pipe smoking was all the rage. The earliest known picture of American pipe smokers was painted by one Jacques Le Moyne de Morgues. An all-around artist, Le Moyne came to Florida with René de Laudonnière's second expedition to Florida to chart the coastline and sketch the natives. Laudonnière's objective was the usual one: gold. His mission was the establishment of a seacoast fort from which to raid Spanish galleons returning from the Indies through the Straits of Florida. A Spanish "task force" was sent to Florida to prevent this, and did, by slaughtering the garrison in 1565; Le Moyne was one of a few who escaped. All but one of his forty-seven paintings were later lost, but not before a Flemish engraver made copies of them. Le Moyne's rendering of the strange, naked smokers was accompanied by this caption:

> ... They also have a plant which the Brazilians call *petum* and the Spaniards *tapaco*. After carefully drying its leaves, they put them in the bowl of a pipe. They light the pipe, and, holding its other end in their mouths, they inhale the smoke so deeply that it comes out through their mouths and noses; by this means they often cure infections.

What became of Le Moyne is not precisely known, except that his rescue ship was swept off course and landed him in England instead of France. From Swansea Bay Le Moyne is supposed to have journeyed to London, married, and become "a servaunt to Sir Walter Raleigh."

Perhaps Le Moyne's paintings and his stories of the New World had something to do with Raleigh's first expedition to Virginia in 1584. But tales about America in general and tobacco in particular were well known in Europe and in England long before Le Moyne escaped the Spaniards' pikes. Only ten years after Columbus, Spanish sailors picked up the art of chewing tobacco from South American Indians and carried the habit back to Spain. Jacques Cartier

8

paddled up the St. Lawrence River in 1535 and reported that "the Indians have a certain herb, of which they lay up a store every Summer, having first dried it in the sun. They always carry some of it in a small bag hanging around their necks. In this bag they also keep a hollow tube of wood or stone. Before using the herb they pound it to powder, which they cram into one end of the tube and plug it with red-hot charcoal. They then suck themselves so full of smoke that it oozes from their mouths like smoke from the flue of a chimney. They say the habit is most wholesome." Unfortunately, Cartier visited North America more than 60 years before the strong, native *Nicotiana rustica* was supplanted by mild *Nicotiana tabacum* from Central and South America: "We found that tobacco bit our tongues like pepper."

Fifteen years after Cartier's tonguebite, Phillip II of Spain—the same ambitious Phillip who was to wipe out Laudonnière's expedition—sent one Francis Hernandez de Toledo on a mission to Mexico. Toledo was the first to bring back living tobacco plants for cultivation in Europe. And in 1561 Jean Nicot, Lord of Villemain and ambassador to Portugal, took some Florida tobacco plants to Paris. They were given to Catharine de Medici, who later learned to like snuff—so much so that the first French name for tobacco was *herbe Medici*. But it was Nicot, the first influential promoter of tobacco, who finally gave his name to the species *Nicotiana tabacum*.

The most famous tobacco promoter, of course, was Sir Walter Raleigh. In establishing the first Virginia colony, he commissioned one Thomas Hariot to spend a year in the New World as surveyor and historian. Hariot returned in 1586 with two related plants—the tobacco and the potato—and a sheaf of notes. The latter were titled "A briefe and true report of the new found land of Virginia: of the commodities there found and to be raised, as well marchantable, as others for victuall, building and other necessarie uses for those that are and shall be the planters there," etc.

Uppowoc

Before the manuscript was even published, Raleigh had planted a patch of tobacco in Ireland, where he was Governor of Kilcolman. The story goes that Sir Walter smoked his first tobacco in Ireland—

Jean Nicot, French ambassador to Portuguese court, sent tobacco to Catharine de Medici. So the plant was at first herbe Medici, then Nicotiana tabacum.

In England, Sir Walter Raleigh was credited with making pipe-smoking a fashion at Queen Elizabeth's court. Tobacco spread to Persia and the Far East.

Wooden Indians were used by London tobacconists to suggest the faraway source of the fragrant leaf. In France, tobacco was sold as a medicine by druggists.

Father of the American tobacco industry was John Rolfe, who smoked Spanish tobacco in his pipe before sailing to Jamestown in 1610. Rolfe noted the biting taste of the native Virginia leaf; he imported West Indian seed to grow a milder variety, exported a shipment in 1613.

Industry's "mother" was Pocahontas, whose marriage to Rolfe established peace between Indians and colonists.

in a pipe, naturally. One reason for his enthusiasm may have been Hariot's original testimonial:

> There is an herb called *uppowoc*, which sows itself. In the West Indies it has several names, according to the different places where it grows and is used, but the Spaniards generally call it tobacco. Its leaves are dried, made into powder, and then smoked by being sucked through clay pipes into the stomach and head. The fumes purge superfluous phlegm and gross humors from the body, but if there are any obstructions it breaks them up. By this means the natives keep in excellent health, without many of the grievous diseases which often afflict us in England.

> This uppowoc is so highly valued by them that they think their gods are delighted with it. Sometimes they make holy fires and cast the powder into them as a sacrifice. If there is a storm on the waters, they throw it up into the air. This is always done with strange gestures and stamping, sometimes dancing, clapping of hands, holding hands up, and staring into the heavens . . .

> While we were there we used to suck in the smoke as they did, and now that we are back in England we still do. We have found many rare and wonderful proofs of the uppowoc's virtues, which would themselves require a volume to relate. There is sufficient evidence in the fact that it is used by so many men and women of great calling, as well as by some learned physicians.

The 1613 shipment sent by John Rolfe from Jamestown was by no means the first to come from the New World. Leaf from the West Indies and from what is now Latin America was reaching Europe frequently in Spanish bottoms. The original Virginia tobacco was a thick-fibered, powerful product, *Nicotiana rustica*. The leaf cultivated by Rolfe and his wife Pocahontas, though much darker than today's "Bright," was an improved strain of *Nicotiana tabacum* whose seed came from the Spanish possessions in Latin America.

Long before Raleigh's death in 1618, tobacco had spread from England to Sweden, Russia and Turkey; from Turkey to Egypt and Persia; from France to Holland; from Portugal to India, Java and China. At the last, when Raleigh had lost favor at Court and was about to lose his head on the scaffold, tobacco remained as "a lone man's companion." Waiting in the Tower of London for the executioner, Raleigh had his last smoke.

Royal blast

It may have been that Raleigh's fondness for smoking contributed to his demise. For the monarch who beheaded him was also the first great tobacco-hater, James I. Quipped one London wag of the King's obsession: "Where there's smoke, there's ire." In his *Counterblaste to Tobacco*, issued in 1604, James blamed smoking for virtually all the sicknesses to which flesh is heir. "And now good Countrey men," thundered he, "let us (I pray you) consider, what honour or policie can move us to imitate the barbarous and beastly manners of the wilde, godlesse, and slavish Indians, especially in so vile and stinking a custome? . . . Why do we not as well imitate them in walking naked as they do?" The cantankerous Tudor was, in fact, the first major obstacle the American tobacco industry had to surmount. That it did was an early proof of the strong attachment the world had—and has—for the fragrant herb.

In many ways, the infant industry, then concentrated in Virginia, faced the same general problems it was later to encounter again and again: heavy taxation, denunciations from puritanical crusaders, negative reactions following exaggerated claims. (In France, the weed was sold only by apothecaries as a medicine, as a result of explorers' wild tales of its "healing qualities.")

Motivated by hatred of Raleigh and of the Spanish who then did most of the commerce in tobacco, James raised the import duty from tuppence per pound to six shillings tenpence. Despite this 4,000% increase—possibly the largest percentage tax boost ever recorded—trade in Virginia leaf flourished. The high duty, naturally, led to smuggling on a wide scale; but it also encouraged the cultivation of tobacco in England itself.

Money crop

In many colonies of the New World, tobacco leaf was legal tender for the payment of wages, debts and taxes. And no wonder. It was the greatest single source of wealth for Virginia, Maryland and eventually North Carolina. Until 1803, when cotton became king, tobacco was the nation's most valuable export commodity. It was, in a double sense, the "makings" of a nation.

Fortunately for the impoverished settlers of

James I of England hated Raleigh, tobacco-shipping Spaniards, and the weed itself. His Counterblaste to Tobacco blamed smoking for all earthly ailments.

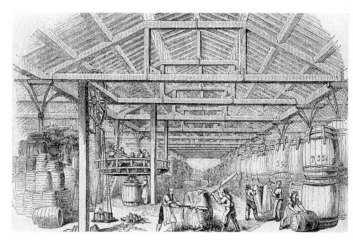

James raised duty on Virginia leaf by 4,000%, but tobacco warehouses thrived on London docks. Imports grew from 20,000 pounds in 1617 to 500,000 in 1628.

European demand made tobacco the foremost commodity of the Virginia and Maryland colonies. For the next two centuries, it was America's No. 1 export.

To keep export quality high, Virginia leaf had to be approved by government inspectors before being sold. Tobacco was kept in bonded public warehouses while negotiations took place with "tobacco notes."

Virginia, the European market for tobacco was well-established before 1607, date of the colony's official founding. Despite the *Counterblaste*, the custom of smoking took London by storm. By 1614 there were 7,000 shops in that city alone which stocked tobacco. And this was only the beginning. In 1617, Virginia shipped 20,000 pounds to England; in 1628, 500,000 pounds; in 1638, 1,400,000 pounds. By 1771, England and Scotland were importing about 102,000,000 pounds a year between them, virtually all from the Chesapeake colonies. This was no mean quantity for the age of wooden, wind-driven bottoms. Total exports 150 years later, for example, were in the neighborhood of 590,000,000 pounds. About half of this was exported through the Virginia ports—most of it in the lighter, milder flue-cured types rather than the colonial "shipping leaf." But the 1771 leaf traffic from the Chesapeake area was considerable, even by present-day standards.

Once the mother country recovered from its disappointment over the lack of New World gold, it set about fencing off its new commerce in tobacco. Tariff walls were thrown up: Virginia Company imports were taxed only half as much as those from Spain. In 1620, cultivation of tobacco in England was prohibited; three years later, England excluded Spanish imports almost entirely. In return for this thoroughgoing protection, the colonists agreed to export tobacco only to England.

One reason for the close control was the matter of internal revenue taxes, based on the firm popularity of smoking. During the century ending with the Treaty of Paris and the birth of a free United States, import duties ran from four to six times the planter's net price—in addition to Virginia's own levy of two shillings on each hogshead of tobacco exported. To complete the parallel with modern times, a crude form of crop control was also practised by the colonial legislatures. At first, second-growth farming was banned and inferior grades were burned; later, a system of inspectors and public warehouses insured that no low-grade leaf was approved for sale. Approved tobacco remained in bond; actual negotiations for it were accomplished through inspectors' receipts. These so-called "tobacco notes" performed the same economic function as the banknotes and greenbacks of the next century.

The Tobacco War

During the Revolution itself, tobacco was doubly important. Virginia leaf was used to pay interest on loans from France and to pay for war materiel. In 1776, the year New York City was lost to the British, General George Washington appealed to his countrymen: "I say, if you can't send money, send tobacco." Washington knew his men and he knew his tobacco: he was one of the larger tobacco planters and exporters of his time. Nor was the strategic value of Virginia leaf lost on the enemy. The 1781 campaign waged by Phillips and Arnold in the Old

Dominion was later recalled as "The Tobacco War," since the British troops seemed more anxious to kill off green tobacco plants than blue-coated Revolutionaries. At the close of the war, Virginia's General Assembly was fixing salaries in terms of leaf tobacco, currency having lost its stability.

After the Revolution, a subtle change in America's smoking habits got under way. Snuff, the modish form of consumption, gave way to chewing, a cheaper and more practical habit for a nation of people on the move. Thus, as in every major shift of tobacco usage, economics played as big a part as fashion.

The Spanish sailors had picked up the chewing habit from South and Central America; from the North American Indians, who were exclusively pipe smokers, the English had taken up the "bright glowing stove." The first tobacconists' Indians, symbolic of the leaf's romantic origin, stood in front of London shops. But as pipe smoking became more "common" and filtered down to the lower classes, the style-setting *haute monde* looked for something more delicate. Snuff-taking became fashionable in Parisian circles, partly because it overcame some ladies' objections to smoke, partly because it enabled other high-born ladies to use tobacco daintily. Snuff had other advantages: it required no tinder-boxes, it carried no danger of fire, it was well suited to the ostentatious display of finger rings and bejeweled boxes. Eventually, the "lust of the longing nose" made its way to England and thence to the Anglo-Saxon high society of the colonies.

The independent smoker

So, after the cord to the mother country was cut, snuff became less popular. It was associated with the hated English dandies and its rejection was, in a way, a declaration of independence. Also, early in the nineteenth century, tobacco ceased to be the prime commodity of export. More of it was consumed at home, by farmers less interested in modishness than in convenience and cheapness. Home-grown tobacco could be taken via the pipe, or simply chewed, and so it was. "Unmanufactured tobacco" was the choice of the unmannered American during the Agrarian Age, lasting until the War Between the States.

Meanwhile the pipe remained as the tradi-

In 1776 the colonies prepared to fight Britain for their independence. General Washington appealed for supplies: "If you can't send money, send tobacco."

In rejecting the mother country, Americans rejected many of its fashions as well. Snuff-taking, a habit associated with British dandies, lost popularity.

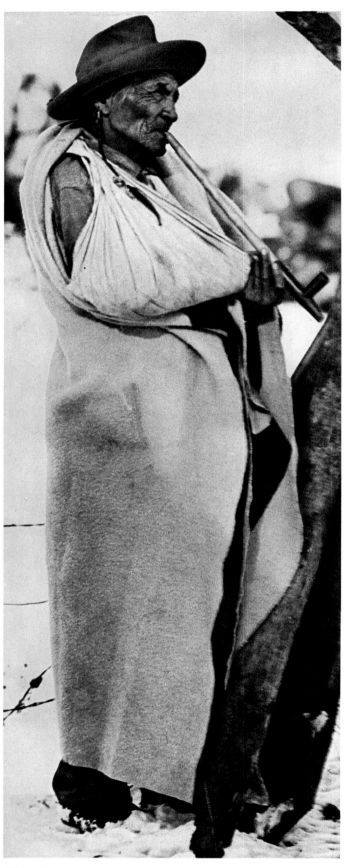

The pipe, called a calumet by Indians, was the old, traditional way to smoke, although chewing tobacco was handier. In 1874, redmen still smoked calumets.

tional smoking instrument. Even the sailors and wanderers who chewed during the day were likely to take an evening pipeful. Just as the calumet or peace-pipe symbolized calm goodwill to the North American Indians, so the polished briar or rough corncob came to mean solace and serenity to his white conquerors. A good deal of fanciful allusion to "the philosophical pipe" entered the literature, but perhaps the most impressive lines were Longfellow's, from *Hiawatha:*

> On the Mountains of the Prairie,
> On the great Red Pipe-Stone Quarry,
> Gitchie Manito, the mighty.
>
> From the red stone of the quarry,
> With his hand he broke a fragment,
> Moulded it into a pipe-head,
> Shaped and fashioned it with figures.
>
> From the margin of the river
> Took a large reed for a pipe-stem,
> With its dark green leaves upon it;
> Filled the pipe with bark of willow,
> With the bark of the red willow.
>
> Break the red stone from this quarry,
> Mould and make it into Peace-Pipes,
> Take the reeds that grow beside you,
> Deck them with our brightest feathers,
> Share the calumet together
> And as brothers live hence forward!

Whether Gitchie Manito ever smoked red willow bark is problematical; the poet, however, was rarely without his sack of *Bull Durham* and is known to have recommended it to many of his friends. Longfellow's manly vision of tobacco as a mystic expression of comradeship was inspired partly by a cigar store Indian which stood before a shop on the Boston-Cambridge road. Made of metal instead of the customary wood, it became known as the "Longfellow Indian," since the poet himself often stopped to admire it. The figure now stands in the Company's New York headquarters.

Regardless of the poetic significance of smoking, the quality of tobacco in the antebellum years was poor. New England grew a harsh, narrow leaf called "shoe-string." The South produced a dark, heavy "shipping leaf" quite different from the light, sweet Bright tobacco raised today. Smoking tobacco and "chaw" were one and the same for many users: it was not until 1864 that White Burley was first grown, a strain distinguished by a remarkable capacity to absorb sugar and flavoring. This Burley, first raised in Ohio and now predominantly a Kentucky and Tennessee product, made possible the manufacture of sweet plug. After the Civil War, it was to revolutionize the smoking and chewing industry; and during World War I it was to revolutionize the cigarette industry. But before 1860, commercial leaf was essentially the same harsh, powerful stuff the early colonists exported. Its enjoyment—except, perhaps, in the form of scented snuff—required a virile palate indeed. This, together with the general turmoil of immigration, westward pioneering and the small size of cities (*i.e.*, the lack of compact primary markets) kept per capita consumption of tobacco from increasing between 1813 and 1870.

The better roll

Americans are not Americans, however, unless they are looking for something better. Among other places, they looked to Cuba, where cigars were being rolled even before the War of Independence. Cigar imports from the Antilles reached the 4,000,000 level by 1804 and the 20,000,000 mark by 1811. And a domestic cigar industry sprang up to give less affluent citizens an imitation of the luxurious imported Havana. The stogie was a roughly rolled smoke of cheap domestic tobacco, tapered only at the mouth end; the cheroot was an even simpler cylinder, open at both ends. The trend was helped by the 1847 campaigns in Mexico, from which American troops returned smoking cigars. Even so, the nation did not become cigar-conscious until the "Brown Decades" following the Civil War, when the imported claro became a symbol of means. At this point, the cigarette appears on the scene.

Powder and smokes

When the paper-rolled cigarette was born is something of a mystery. Many tobacco chroniclers place its birth in 1832, when the Egyptians were laying siege to the Turkish city of Acre. A cannoneer, the legend goes, improved his rate of fire by rolling his powder in paper tubes or "pistils"; his commander, pleased, sent a gift of tobacco to the gun crew. Since a Turkish ball had shattered the only available pipe, the Egyptian soldiers proceeded to smoke the tobacco rolled in the powder paper. The

Longfellow's lines on the peace pipe were inspired partly by this tobacconist's Indian, which stands in the New York headquarters of American Tobacco.

practise soon caught on. Only eleven years later France made cigarette manufacture a government monopoly. But even at that late date (1843), the cigarette was virtually unknown in England. There is a literary reference in that year to "paper cigars," and in an 1854 letter Charles Dickens asked a British friend to send him cigarettes, although he may have used that word to refer to small cigars. The new form of smoking attained world-wide notice after the Crimean War (1854-56), when English officers picked up the "papalete" from their Turkish, French and Italian allies.

In the beginning, every cigarette, even in the salons of London, was a "roll your own" type; it was not until 1866 that "tailor-mades" were turned out in England and the U. S. They were, of course, hand-rolled. Most were larger than present-day cigarettes, and all were made from "Turkish" tobacco, grown in Greece and Bulgaria as well as Turkey.

The Turkish cigarette, as any *Melachrino* smoker can testify, is a unique smoke. Its scent is rich, foreign, exotic. At first, the only market of consequence in America was in New York, with its large foreign-born population. And because hand-rolling required a great deal of labor, New York with its pool of workers was the logical manufacturing site.

But the rise of the cigarette was based on nothing so fortuitous as the chance flight of a Turkish cannonball at Acre. Nor were the *beaux* of London sufficiently influential to generate a new industry on this side of the Atlantic. Just as tobacco itself had sprung from the soil of the New World, so the cigarette was to dominate the entire world's smoking tastes by reason of a specific patch of American earth. In 1838, the first crop of a tobacco which cured to a bright yellow was raised in the sandy, porous soil of Caswell County, North Carolina. First used in cigars, it was a leaf of exceptional sweetness and fine texture. From this little ridge of sandy soil came the American cigarette, now by all odds the smoking standard of the globe. From it, too, came The American Tobacco Company.

In the colonies tobacco was trundled to the market in hogsheads rolled along "tobacco roads." For two *and a half centuries this method of leaf transport continued unchanged: this woodcut is dated 1869.*

PRO BONO PUBLICO

CHARLES KINGSLEY, the English adventure novelist, described tobacco as "a lone man's companion, a bachelor's friend, a hungry man's food, a sad man's cordial, a wakeful man's sleep, and a chilly man's fire." If Kingsley was correct, it is entirely logical that the great shifts in tobacco fashion should follow wars. For soldiers are lonely, hungry, sad, wakeful, chilly; and they live, perforce, like bachelors. Since the days of Marco Polo, soldier-adventurers have been the great diffusers of invention, of language, of custom. Returned to civil life from their travels and travails, they become the nucleus of what economists call "the consuming public."

It was on the receding tidal wave of a great war that Washington Duke of North Carolina launched his tobacco business. He was a serious and thrifty man who had attained a 300-acre farm four miles north of Durham and four children: Brodie by his first wife; Benjamin, Mary and James by a second. A widower, Duke did not enter the Confederate army until 1863; he was captured in the retreat from Richmond before Lee surrendered at Appomattox Court House. In 1865 the forty-five-year-old veteran was released from Libby Prison and sent to New Bern, North Carolina, 137 miles from home. Having only 50c in hard cash, obtained from a Federal soldier in exchange for a five-dollar Confederate bill, he walked the 137 miles.

The farm had been ransacked by Federal troops, except for a little Bright tobacco leaf and some flour. To raise working capital Duke sold his land and rented back a few acres of it. After sending for his children, whom their grandparents had kept, he pulverized and cleaned the tobacco in a small log barn. Packed in muslin bags labeled *Pro Bono Publico*,* it was loaded onto a wagon drawn by two blind mules. Reins in hand, Duke rattled east toward Raleigh, sleeping by the roadside at night and cooking his own food in a frying pan—bacon, corn meal, sweet potatoes. The expedition was a success. Duke exchanged his flour for cotton, which he sold in Raleigh; part of the proceeds went into a present for his children—a bag of brown sugar. (Buck, the youngest, ate so much of it that he lost his "sweet tooth" for the rest of his life.) More important, the tobacco found a ready cash market, and yielded enough money to buy a supply of bacon.

The ready market for Duke's tobacco was not entirely a local one. Shortly after the surrender at Appomattox, General Joe Johnston and 30,000 Con-

*Which, translated, means "for the good of the public."

Before World War I cigarette sales were relatively minor. Plug, identified with tin tags, was the big seller.

federate troops retreated from Raleigh and passed through Durham in their pell-mell westward flight. Their pursuer, General William Tecumseh Sherman, first sent his cavalry into Durham and later came himself to discuss a truce with Johnston. Thus both Federal and Confederate troops were "stationed," so to speak, in Durham, long enough to sample tobacco from the Golden Belt. (Although tobacco rations for both Federal and Confederate troops were authorized, it appears that they left considerable to be desired in quality and in regularity of issue.) By 1865, the Caswell County yellow leaf had spread to Person, Warren, Orange, Granville and Rockingham – now the heart of the Bright tobacco region – and Durham was the manufacturing center for it. One factory which turned out *Best Flavored Spanish Smoking Tobacco* was cleaned out by the Federals. Its proprietor, John Green, first thought he was ruined; but the raid was a blessing in disguise. After they were mustered out, the Federal soldiers remembered the fine smoking tobacco made in Durham and began to send orders for it. So, in time, did such notables as James Russell Lowell, Henry Wadsworth Longfellow, Alfred Lord Tennyson and Thomas Carlyle.

Eventually, Green's mixture was renamed *Genuine Durham Smoking Tobacco*, with a bull's picture between "Genuine" and "Durham." When Green died in 1869, a former tobacco retailer named Blackwell bought the *Bull Durham* business. He and his successor advertised heavily, and Durham soon became "the town renowned the world around." The W. T. Blackwell Company for a time commanded the

tobacco industry of Durham; and like every other local tobacco man, Washington Duke considered "the Bull Factory" his major competition.

Bull Fight

The extent of *Bull Durham's* vogue can best be appreciated by the number of its imitators, which came onto the market in a steady stream during the 1870s. All used the rectangular bronze-on-black label. There was *Sitting Bull Durham* (!) garnished with a sketch of that worthy Sioux medicine man. There were *Durham Gold Leaf, Magic Durham, Jersey Bull, El Burro, The DURHAM Smoking Tobacco, Pride of Durham, Billy Boy DURHAM* (made in Rochester), *Black Bull, Dream DURHAM, Nickel-Plated Durham* and *Dime Durham*. One local manufacturer, Morris & Son, tried a variant of the original Blackwell name – *Eureka Spanish Flavored Durham*. Another firm, F. W. Felgner of Baltimore, had several entries in the Bull ring: *Stokes vs. Durham*, whose label showed a lady bullfighter spearing a Spanish bull, *Globe Durham, Steer, Bully, Buffalo, Wild Buffalo* and *Buffalo Bill*. By the time the last of these were registered in 1876, imitation bulls were "old hat" – the latter, ironically, being one of Felgner's own smoking tobacco brands. Gail & Ax carried the Spanish theme a step further with *Los Toros Tobaco de Fumar*. And as late as 1878 Wilkens of Baltimore weighed in with *Old Bull, Bull's Head, Bison* and *The Brindle*. Although Washington Duke's early labels were printed in bronze on glossy black, he stubbornly refused to ape the Bull. *Duke of Durham* smoking tobacco bore

the image of a pipe-smoking nobleman, and the *Pro Bono Publico* label kept its 1868 format, showing an Indian chief smoking a calumet next to a cask of "Duke's Durham Tobacco," with a small caption reading "Do this."

In view of *Bull Durham*'s dominance, it seems rather remarkable that a penniless ex-Johnny Reb should start out from scratch to give it battle. To the forty-five-year-old Duke, however, the tobacco business had certain obvious advantages. With the slaves emancipated and no cash to lay out for wages, a man and his sons could grow, flail, bag and sell tobacco all by themselves. And with Blackwell's advertising making Durham products world-renowned, the market was growing. Using first the log cabin, then a stable, and later a frame building right on their farm, W. Duke and Sons turned out 15,000 pounds of product in their first full year, 1866. At 30c or 40c per pound after revenue taxes, this brought in about $5,000. The brand name was still *Pro Bono Publico*. In 1869 Brodie Duke, the eldest son, moved into an old two-story building in Durham where he made (1) his own meals and (2) a brand of smoking tobacco called *Semper Idem* and, beginning in 1871, *Duke of Durham*.

Five years later the four Dukes were together again in their own Durham factory, a false-fronted affair on Main Street topped off with a cupola. But *Duke of Durham* was no match for *Bull Durham*, and young James Buchanan Duke, then in charge of manufacturing, came to a decision. "My company," he told a local lawyer, "is up against a stone wall. It can not compete with the Bull. Something has to be done and that quick. As for me, I am going into the cigarette business." In 1881, he did.

Bonsacks and taxes

Thinking big was Buck Duke's lifelong characteristic, and he started acting big in 1881, at the age of twenty-four. Loth to experiment with cigarette manufacture, he brought a factory manager and skilled rollers from New York. Shortly thereafter a Virginian, James Bonsack, invented a making machine said to reduce manufacturing costs from 80c per thousand to 30c. The leading cigarette firms—Allen and Ginter of Richmond, Kimball of Rochester, Kinney, and Goodwin, both of New York City—hesitated to lease Bonsack's maker. They felt consumers would resent the replacement of hand-rolled cigarettes by machine products.

In view of the machine's riskiness and unproved performance, Duke contracted to use Bonsacks at a royalty of 24c per thousand rather than 30c. (Later a clause guaranteed that Duke's royalty should always be 25% less than the standard rental.) It turned out that two machines Bonsack delivered were not efficient, but with the help of a brilliant young mechanic named William O'Brien, Duke was able to improve them to turn out 200 cigarettes a minute (today's machines have a top speed of 1,600 and a "cruising speed" of about 1,300).

Manufacturing taken care of, Duke turned his attention to packaging and invented the slide-and-shell box. This done, he narrowed his profit margins

From Richmond's Libby Prison, once a tobacco plant, Washington Duke returned to Durham in 1865. On his ravaged farm, only an old pile of tobacco remained.

In a tiny log cabin, Duke and his young sons beat the tobacco, labeled it Pro Bono Publico, sold it from a wagon. The leaf was good; so was business.

Decision to make cigarettes was made by young Buck Duke in 1881. Three years later, Buck went to New York City, then the heart of the cigarette market.

to the minimum in anticipation of mechanization savings. Ten *Duke of Durham* cigarettes were sold for a nickel, compared with the then-standard price of 10c. In this, young Duke was helped by a reduction in the government tax from $1.75 to 50c a thousand. The new rate became effective in 1883, just before the Bonsack machines achieved full efficiency.

Given these factors — choice leaf, efficient manufacture, the right price — only the problem of merchandising remained. Duke's sales chief, Richard H. Wright, spent almost two years in Europe, Africa, India, Australia and New Zealand. Other salesmen opened up domestic markets by selling jobbers and retailers, doubled in brass by reporting on the buying public's reactions to the various brands. In 1884, Duke himself went to New York, established a loft factory there on Rivington Street, personally canvassed the retail trade, invested heavily in billboard and newspaper advertisements, devised sales lures like the premium coupon and the celebrity picture, one in every package. The pictures, mostly of actresses and athletes, came in numbered sets to provide an extra incentive for repeat buying. For seventy-five coupons, a Duke customer could obtain a folding album depicting the country's reigning beauties in color. During the day he watched over his manufacturing operation, seeing that his cigarettes were tightly rolled and well-packaged in the slide-and-shell boxes. At night he would make the rounds, counting discarded cigarette boxes on the street to gauge progress of the various brands. At first he lived in Harlem, but the long commute seemed a waste of time and he moved to a two-dollar-a-week hall bedroom in the Bowery.

Major Ginter's mistake

The simultaneous exercise of Duke's foresight in all these directions added up to a management *tour de force.* In 1880, before he made his cigarette move, the four leading firms did about 80% of the nation's business, totaling around 409,000,000 cigarettes. By 1889, annual production was 2,152,000,000, of which the Duke firm did 38%, the other four splitting the remainder. During that year Duke approached Major Lewis Ginter to talk merger, was told: "Listen, Duke, you couldn't buy us out to save your neck. You haven't enough money and you

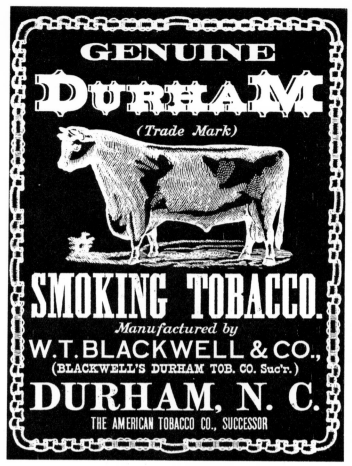

The curing of light, yellow tobacco in the Old Belt made Durham tobacco famous. Demand for the flue-cured product soared during and after the Civil War; any tobacco marked "Durham" was readily received. Thus, actual Durham makers took pains to use "genuine" on

their labels. Bellwether brand was Bull Durham, its trademark supposedly inspired by that of a mustard made in Durham, England. First brand of W. Duke, an enterprise later to grow into American Tobacco, was Pro Bono Publico, a granulated tobacco sold in bags.

couldn't borrow enough." Ginter was wrong on both counts. Buck Duke was widening his market with Ginter's own specialty, advertising—$800,000 worth in 1889, or about 96¢ per thousand cigarettes. His four big rivals lacked both his zest and his talent. In 1890, they joined forces with W. Duke Sons and Company to create a new corporation, capitalized at $25 million. The President was, of course, James Buchanan Duke; the name of the new firm, The American Tobacco Company.

The brand names on the books of the new company were almost too numerous to count. Connorton's Tobacco Brand Directory had listed only 108 cigarette names in its 1885 edition, published in Chicago. Among the entries were such shudder-producing appellations as *Catarrh, Hunkidori* and *Old Rip.* The more important brands included Allen and

Ginter's *Dubec, Bon Ton, Matchless* and *Napoleons,* along with *Old Rip* (Van Winkle); Goodwin's *Canvas Back, Old Judge* and *Welcome;* Kimball's *Cloth of Gold, Fragrant Vanity Fair, Turkish Orientals, Old Gold,* and *Three Kings.* Kinney had the renowned *Sweet Caporal* brand, still made by The American Tobacco Company. Virtually all were straight Bright tobacco smokes, although the "Sweet Caps" were thought to contain a seasoning of Turkish leaf.

To this array Duke brought the *Duke of Durham* brand, *Cyclone, Cameo, Cross Cut* and *Duke's Best,* the last four introduced in cigarette form when he invaded New York in 1884. *Cyclone* was labeled "Everything in quality, but little expended for decoration." Other Duke cigarettes included *Pedro, Town Talk* and *Pin Head,* the latter bearing the proud inscription, "These cigarettes are manufactured on

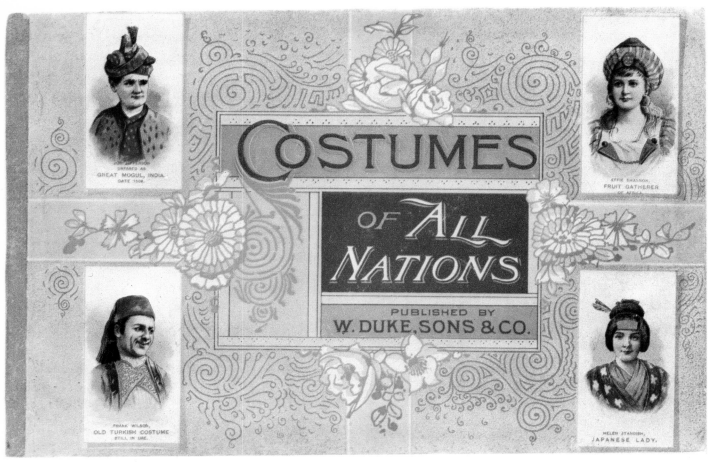

In 1888, when the Dukes offered this premium album, advertising was a package deal. Redeemable coupons were big buying incentives. Duke varied these with billboard and poster ads to presell his new brands.

the Bonsack Cigarette Machine." Before 1898, the *Cycle* brand was labeled "The best that can be made for the money," and after that year the package further emphasized economy in these capital letters: "1 BOX OF 10 FOR 3 CENTS–2 BOXES OF 10 FOR 5 CENTS." Prominent among the early American Tobacco cigarette brands, as distinct from the Duke brands, were *Fair Play*, *Battle Ax*, *Motor*, *Colonial* and *Indian Head*, the last bearing the Powhatan trademark. The original smoking tobacco, *Pro Bono Publico*, was still being made, and the original Duke was still seriously living up to that dignified phrase: in the early 1890s, having passed threescore and ten, he devoted himself to local affairs. His most prominent activity was the bringing of Trinity College to Durham. Following his initial contribution of $85,000, Washington Duke and his sons continued to invest in the school, which soon became the largest endowed college in the Southeast. The last and largest gift of $40 million was made by James B.

Duke in 1924, when Trinity College became Duke University.

But in the first year of American Tobacco, Buck Duke's investments were strictly along business lines. The first prize on his list, the National Tobacco Works of Louisville, was acquired in 1891. National was famous for plug, particularly its *Piper Heidsieck* brand (still sold by The American Tobacco Company). Its purchase by American moved the Drummond company to cut the price of its cheap brand: Duke answered by pricing *Battle Ax* at a penny less, and a round of plug plugging followed.* As a result Drummond, Lorillard, Mayo and several lesser com-

---

*As in the case of *Bull Durham*, competition in plug was often nearly synonymous with imitation. *Piper Heidsieck* was registered as a tobacco brand in December of 1882 by Pfingst, Doerhoefer & Company, which later became the National Tobacco Works of Louisville. Inevitably, a *Mumm's Extra Dry* plug was registered in 1884 by a small manufacturer in nearby Covington, Kentucky.

panies were bought. In 1898 Duke's large stock-holders persuaded him to head a subsidiary, Continental Tobacco, newly incorporated to handle the plug lines. At the time this was a far more important consolidation than the five-sided cigarette merger of 1890. The greatest part of tobacco consumed, in pounds if not in dollar value, was chewed. Nor was plug a lowbrow or even a middlebrow commodity: every man of parts, from ex-president Grover Cleveland to the executive in his city office, was equipped with a personal cuspidor. But although American Tobacco achieved 60% of plug sales by the last of the gay nineties, the manufactured-tobacco market itself increased only 2%. By contrast, the cigarette was going through a riotous proliferation of brands. New factories sprang up in every city, and production increased 26% in the ten years ended 1899.

It was Duke's preoccupation with the plug

trade that finally led to the purchase of his old nemesis, Blackwell's *Bull Durham*. A group of New York financiers had bought control of the old Blackwell company, and, aware of Duke's interest in plug, an option on an interest in a St. Louis plugmaker, Liggett and Myers. In addition the New York group, operating as the Union Tobacco Company, had taken over National Cigarette and Tobacco Company of New York, an important cigarette manufacturer. Duke bought Union at a price requiring the issue of new common stock: $12.5 million in American common was exchanged for $3 million in cash and the securities of Union.

It would be a mistake, however, to assume that Duke's purchases revolved only around tangible assets like plants or intangible assets like brand names (book-valued, in 1890, at $20 million of The American Tobacco Company's $25 million asset worth). Tall,

Premiums were silk flags or pictures. Lithographs of Mrs. Langtry (left) and Lillian Russell were in

the costume album; smaller ones were slipped into cigarette boxes, numbered to induce "chain buying."

red-haired, austere, J. B. Duke was then a handler of men, a professional executive rather than a financier. He owned far less than a controlling interest in American Tobacco common. In 1897 Colonel Oliver Payne of Standard Oil cornered a working majority of the stock, and Duke told Payne he would sell his shares and start a new company if Payne's group desired it. Payne backed down and gave Duke a free hand from that point onward. Not that Duke was "agin'" the men who furnished capital: in fact, his principal motive in buying Union was to bring into the American camp such well-connected men as Thomas Fortune Ryan, William C. Whitney, Anthony H. Brady and P. A. B. Widener. Along with Blackwell's battle-tested *Bull Durham* brand, Duke secured the services of its manager, a Philadelphian named Percival S. Hill. The latter quickly became American's Vice President in charge of sales, and eventually brought his son, George Washington Hill, into the corporation.

By now, Buck Duke's operating formula was apparent to his rivals. Its essence was volume first, profits second. The *modus operandi:* (1) devise a superior product; (2) hire the best people to make it; (3) price it as low as possible; (4) mechanize, organize, merchandise. This strategy, abetted by premium giveaways, led to a volume great enough to compensate for the low profit margin per unit of sale. It also gave Duke's products a lasting market, as contrasted with the sporadic demand for the high-priced, high-margined specialties on which less foresighted manufacturers pinned their hopes. Duke's methods, of course, were not uniquely his. The improvements in quality-controlling machinery and in national communication which made volume possible were being adopted by the smartest managements in meat-packing, in oil, in lead, in sugar, in whiskey, in cottonseed-oil, in copper, in cordage. The Rockefellers, the Carnegies and the rest soon were to dominate their respective industries, and their head starts in the new producing and selling methods led inevitably to monopolies. Despite the legal penalties later imposed on such leadership, the new concept of big business was to continue and create a new national economy, greater than any the world had ever seen. In the wars of the twentieth century, concentrated volume production was to prove the nation's most

Until 1883, cigarettes were handmade. This pretty roller in Allen & Ginter's Richmond factory made four cigarettes a minute. Machines now make 1,600.

indispensable military asset. And during the intervals of peace, the new "brand land" showed a rising standard of living that is still the envy of the world.

Plug and nickels

In 1900, however, neither James Buchanan Duke nor his industrial contemporaries could foresee all this. Duke was, in fact, gravely concerned about his cigarette business. Since 1897, the nation's consumption of cigarettes had dropped off each year. A big reason was the tax, which had gone from 50¢ to $1.00 per thousand in 1897, thence to $1.50 in 1898. One of Continental's nickel brands, *Cycle*, was unable to hold the price line and dropped from 600,000,000 to 40,000,000 sales in two years. The other inexpensive brands, which had shown the steepest increase during the nineties, suffered similarly when odd pennies were added to the price. Furthermore, cigarette distribution was by no means

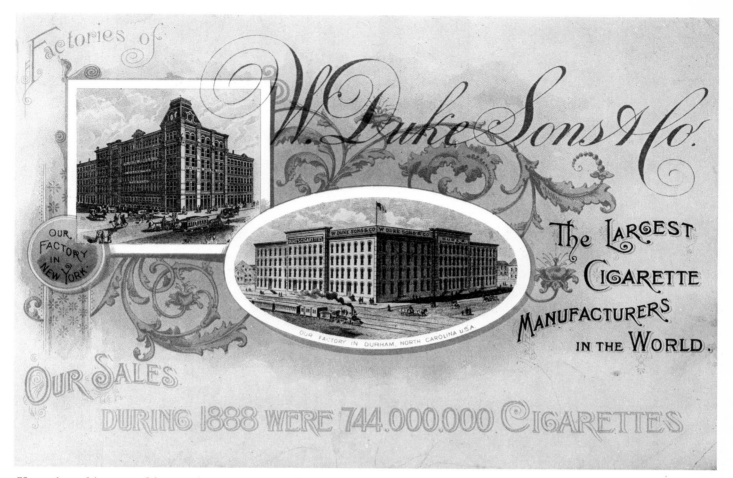

Use of making machines, along with improved leaf quality and aggressive advertising, enabled Duke to win more than a third of cigarette sales by 1889.

But mechanization also increased the cigarette market as a whole—from about 640,000,000 units in 1883, the first machine year, to about 2,152,000,000 by 1889.

national; Duke himself may have wondered whether they represented a big-city fashion, possibly a passing one. This suspicion appeared to be confirmed by the gains registered by his top smoking tobacco, *Duke's Mixture.* This was the old *Pro Bono Publico,* renamed in 1889 as a challenge to Blackwell's *Bull Durham.* The brand jumped from 3,600,000 to 5,500,000 pounds between 1896 and 1897—the very year that cigarette sales began to soften. Even after the Bull was brought into American's brand stable, *Duke's Mixture* continued to grow, topping the 11,000,000-pound mark by 1900. With the bulk of the tobacco business still in cigars and manufactured (smoking and chewing) leaf,* Duke turned to them.

The previous year, Duke had reinforced his

---

*In 1904, when the new American Tobacco Company was formed, cigarettes accounted for only 5c of the consumer's tobacco dollar. Cigars accounted for 60c, chewing and smoking tobacco for 33c, snuff for 2c.

plug position by investing heavily in a small but prospering business in Winston-Salem, owned by Richard Joshua Reynolds. The limited financial resources of Winston-Salem could not supply the expansion capital Reynolds needed, and in 1899 he re-incorporated in New Jersey. American held a two-thirds interest in the reorganized Reynolds company, but played no part in its actual operation. One reason was the unique character of Reynolds' principal product, flat plug; another was the stubborn individuality of Josh Reynolds himself, who resented his dependence on Northern capital. One historian quotes him with this apology: "Sometimes you have to join hands with a fellow to keep him from ruining you and to get the under hold yourself." Another small firm permitted to operate more or less autonomously after American bought it out was Lorillard. That company contributed lines of plug, smoking tobacco and snuff.

Tobacco was emerging as a big business throughout the world. In Great Britain, whose demand for the Virginia leaf first made tobacco a staple, smoking flourished in all its forms. The extent of tobacco manufacture in England is suggested by this woodcut of Cope & Company's huge cigar factory in Liverpool.

During the eighties and nineties, tin tags pronged into plug tobacco served the same function as fancy embossed bands did for cigars: they lent individuality. During the early 1900s they constituted important sales incentives, for the tags were redeemable at an average penny-and-a-half per pound (sometimes in cash, sometimes in prizes). In 1902, a year in which the organization sold 132,600,000 pounds of plug tobacco, the "tin-tag fund" was credited with over $2,000,000. Of this, $1,567,000 was spent in redeeming tags and the rest returned to the income account. Other funds provided for redemption of coupons or box fronts from cigarettes (especially *Sweet Caporal*), little cigars, and pipe tobacco.

By the turn of the century, then, American Tobacco had about three-fifths of the nation's smoking and chewing tobacco business. The twentieth century's first year also saw the organization of American Snuff Company. The new subsidiary took over the snuff-making assets of Lorillard, the George W. Helme Company, and Atlantic Snuff, together with Continental Tobacco's accumulation of lesser snuff properties. Although American Snuff began with 80% of the U. S. market, snuff sales were not only negligible but declining. The product was a full two centuries past its heyday of fashion; it was no longer sniffed but rather "dipped," that is, applied between gum and cheek with a stick dipped into the container. By its transfer from nostril to mouth snuff lost all its original *hauteur* and became merely a variant of straight "eatin' tobacco." In this form it still retains a small loyal clientele among outdoor workers and employees of factories where smoking is prohibited.

In 1890, when Duke's four big rivals joined him to form the first American Tobacco Company, machines and mass advertising were creating big businesses.

A Cleveland oilman named Rockefeller was organizing the Standard Oil Trust, and a little Scot, Andrew Carnegie, ruled the world's greatest steel empire.

Duke was strongly attracted to another great prize: the cigar trade. Sales of this most aristocratic and most expensive form of tobacco increased a cool 62% between 1890, when the old American Tobacco Company was organized, and 1904, when the new

corporation was formed. The strength of the market is best indicated by the fact that 6,700,000,000 cigars were consumed in 1903—more than the total bought in 1953. When allowance is made for the increase in population, per capita consumption in the earlier year

Capital to expand American Tobacco came from such financiers as P.A.B. Widener, Anthony Brady, W.C. Whitney. James Duke owned less than a controlling

interest, but no one else could run the business. When one financier bought control, Duke squelched him by threatening to resign and start a new firm.

Cigar box art during the late 19th century ran the gamut from the naive to the sophisticated. Joyful nymphs and reluctant satyr on the inside label of

American Cigar's Hoffman House cigar boxes suggested the famous painting by Bouguereau which hung in the Hoffman House Bar, rendezvous of actors and notables.

was about eighty-four, compared to a recent average of thirty-eight. To put it another way: more than two cigars were smoked in 1903 for every cigarette consumed.

The cigar, Duke found, was a smoking roll of a different color, quite apart from its dark wrapping. It was essentially a handmade item (even today the

machine has not completely replaced the human being in its bunching, shaping, binding, wrapping, and boxing). This being so, there was no economic reason for a large, aggressive organization to dominate cigar making. So the American Cigar Company never achieved more than one-sixth of the nation's cigar trade, although it did become the largest manu-

At the top of the line were such imported Havanas as Villar y Villar. Its boxes were ornamented by this rather complicated but very dignified steel engraving.

From the first, Cremo was one of the popular five-cent brands of American Cigar (as was Hoffman House). Its inside label bore this commercial lithograph, in color.

Anna Held was a five-cent cigar, one of a score of nickel brands sold by American Cigar in its first decade under John B. Cobb and Percival S. Hill.

Caswell Club ranked among the finest of domestic cigars. Brands in this "in-between" class showed less staying power than the more expensive Havanas.

facturer shortly after its founding in 1901. In 1912, when Allie Sylvester succeeded Percy Hill as its president, American Cigar had 40 domestic and 20 Cuban factories and employed 37,000 people. (While the number of cigar-making enterprises has dwindled considerably, from an estimated 20,000 in 1911 to about 1,500 at present, no manufacturer has a very great share of the market. In 1953, for example, the three largest cigar manufacturers—one of which was

The American Tobacco Company—accounted for only 27% of the business among them.) Because it did not lend itself to volume production by machine, and because most retail sales were in units rather than in packs, the cigar was not a very profitable item. In fact, Duke's cigar subsidiary lost $3.5 million in 1902 while doing 16.4% of the nation's cigar business. Net profit on cigar sales of $154 million during 1902-1908 totaled only $1.9 million—1.2%.

Antonio y Cleopatra, always a clear Havana, was "made expressly for persons of taste." Its label is still embossed in gold, printed in four colors.

By 1912, when Allie L. Sylvester became president, American Cigar was bigger than its parent Company, employed 37,000 employees in sixty cigar factories.

In 1891 American bought National Tobacco Works of Louisville, maker of famous Piper Heidsieck plug. Drummond, Mayo and other plug companies followed.

Like cigars, plug comprised a rich, often sweetened filler in a smooth wrapper leaf. It came in twists or blocks, the latter being shaped in wood molds.

The manager of National Tobacco (second from left, seated) was a man of standing. Company's main item was plug, and Mr. Pfingst was a major plugmaker.

Low profit or no, cigar brands seem to live longer than other tobacco forms. Brands like *Anna Held* and *Caswell Club*, popular during the early 1900s, were to hang on until War II production limitations forced their discontinuance.

It was not long before J. B. Duke was looking for new worlds to conquer. And the new world, in his case, was the Old World—more particularly, Britain. Ever since R. H. Wright's globe-girdling sales junket in 1884, the Company had been the major force in cigarette exports. But most of these were cheap cigarettes sent to the Orient; high tariff walls kept the Dukes out of Britain for all practical (*i.e.*, profitable) purposes. In 1901, therefore, American Tobacco purchased a Liverpool tobacco maker, Ogdens, Ltd., with an eye to securing a share of the British market. The English response was immediate and frantic: thirteen large firms combined as the Imperial Tobacco Company, lowered their prices to meet Duke's, and initiated a vigorous "Don't Buy American" campaign. After a year, the two sides called a truce. Duke agreed to stay out of the United Kingdom, while Imperial agreed to stay out of the U. S., Puerto Rico, and Cuba; a new corporation, British-American Tobacco Company—two thirds American-owned, one third British—was formed to do the export business of both companies elsewhere. From the Carlton Hotel on London's Pall Mall, Duke cabled his father in Durham: "I have just completed a great deal with British manufacturers, covering the world, securing great benefit to our companies." (Twenty-six years later American Tobacco was to re-enter the English industry with the purchase of J. Wix & Sons, Limited, a London corporation which now makes *Kensitas* and *Bar One* cigarettes for the United Kingdom market.)

The Turkish rush

Despite Duke's impressive start in smoking tobacco, chew, cigars and snuff, these branches of the trade had gone about as far as they could go. Cigars and chew were well past their peaks, as measured by per-capita consumption, by 1904; smoking tobacco and snuff were to reach peak use during World War I, but showed very little increase after 1900. It was the cigarette, after all, that was to win the nation's smokers. Total sales, which in 1901 had dropped to about the 1890 level, turned up again in 1902. It was certainly no coincidence that the tax of $1.50 per thousand was reduced in that year—to 54c on brands wholesaling under $2.00 per thousand, to $1.08 on more expensive types. But as always, it was the public which foreshadowed the new uptrend. A number of small New York manufacturers—mostly men of Greek, Turkish or Egyptian origin—were concentrating their efforts on all-Turkish cigarettes. Many were retailers who hand-rolled the aromatic Turkish smokes in back rooms. In the five years from 1899 through 1903, their combined sales jumped from 200,000,000 to 750,000,000 cigarettes, the latter figure representing a full fourth of the cigarette market.

Duke made his move, but not too quickly. In addition to the development of straight Turkish brands, some purchased and some begun from scratch, the Company broadened its line to include Turkish-Virginia blends, making possible a compromise between the very high price of Turkish leaf and the more modest cost of domestic tobacco. Among these blends were *Hassan*, *Mecca* and *Fatima*. At the same time a new all-domestic cigarette, *Piedmont*, was brought out, and the new entry soon passed *Sweet Caporal* as the No. 1 seller. In just two years, 1902 and 1903, The American Tobacco Company's Turkish sales climbed to about 370,000,000, or half the independents' total. At the same time the new Turkish blends, some made in oval shape and all festooned with Oriental names and package designs, pushed Duke's sales of inexpensive cigarettes above the two billion mark.

Although the Turks came on with a rush, they were essentially what are sometimes called "big-city cigarettes": fads which die out fairly quickly and whose demand springs more from novelty than from the taste of the broad American public. Because they achieve insignificant volume, such passing fancies are rarely a bargain either for consumer or producer. During the Oriental rage of 1900-1910, the profit margin on American Tobacco's straight Turkish brands was never as great as that on its domestic blends, although the former sold from 10c to 25c per box of ten, compared with 5c for the latter. The lesson in volume economies then learned by Duke has stuck with the Company through the years following. Although some of the turn-of-the-century Turkish

In 1898 there were hundreds of cigarette brands on the market. Duke's originals—Cameo, Crosscut and Cyclone—were still made, though trebling of federal excise taxes from 1c to 3c played hob with the old nickel price. As shown by Cycle's registration in Hawaii, even nickel brands got global distribution.

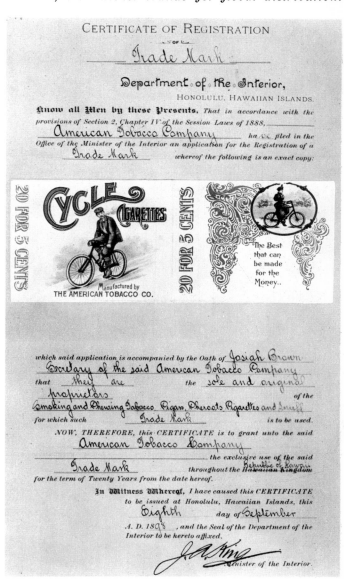

31

brands are still made by American Tobacco out of deference to the habits of longtime customers— *Egyptian Prettiest, Egyptienne Straights, Melachrino, Natural,* and the straight Turkish *Pall Mall*—the great effort has always been spent on national brands.

No brand's land

But as yet, in spite of Duke's mighty efforts to rear a great corporation, there were no truly all-American tobacco products except, perhaps, *Bull Durham.* Connorton's Directory for 1903 listed no fewer than 9,005 brands of plug and twist, 3,625 fine cut chewing tobaccos, 7,046 smoking tobaccos, 3,646 different kinds of snuff and 2,124 "cigarettes, cigarros and cheroots." Tobacco manufacturers were listed in every city of any size. The typical brand could hope for a localized market only, and a firm with national aspirations like American Tobacco simply multiplied the number of its brands to get more business.

In theory, this vast profusion of brands was aimed to please every variation of consumer psychology. Some had nostalgic appeal, like the Louisville cheroot named *Befoe de War.* One wonders, however, what kind of merchandising theory explained such brands as *Bogaboo, Coal Smoke, Corn*

Treasury Department in American Tobacco's Broadway office looked like this during the nineties. Late in the decade Union Tobacco bought out the Blackwell company along with Bull Durham, and American bought Union. After 35 years the Bull had become the most famous of brands, flattered by numerous imitations.

Under amplecheeked President Cleveland the U. S. was a tobacco-chewing nation. No public place, even the busy Wall Street broker's office, lacked cuspidors.

By 1903 a new fad for Turkish cigarettes had swept 25% of the market. Some cigar store Indians became Turks. Duke brought out Turkish blends like Mecca.

Husk, Gloomy Gus, Jack the Giant Killer, Pigs Foot, Peoria Sweepers, Straw Board and Total Eclipse. There was a Wah Hoo smoking tobacco made by Finzer of Louisville, and an implausibly-named T & B brand put up by one George Tuckett of Danville, Virginia, and Hamilton, Canada. Gail & Ax had a Black Horse Infantry brand whose label pictured two pink babes on a black pony. Elder, Dempster sold a plug called Catch Me Willie, complete with a beautiful lithograph of a bosomy maiden eloping from her second-story window. Another smoking tobacco, "patented" ten years before, was called Dental. According to its package, Dental cured "Asthma, Neuralgia, Bad-Colds; Toothache, Headache, Catarrh, Deodorizes the Breath & Preserves the Teeth." Its trademark was a large denture, and its manufacturer, incredible as it sounds, was a Martinsville, Virginia,

company named English, Belcher. A brand of stogies was called Mayer Rat Tail and another Detroit Sweepers (the latter, quixotically, made in Columbus, Ohio). Sen-sen was the name of a cigarette made in Richmond; Quaker Oats cigarettes were made in McSherrystown, Pennsylvania. And a Pittsburgh firm, Dilworth Bros., was turning out a toby—a long, slender, cheap cigar—under the brand name Lucky Strike.

Many of the 2,000-odd cigarette brands were credited to subsidiaries of American Tobacco operating under their own names. Some brands were made by more than one firm, indicating an early disregard for the sanctity of the trademark. An exception to this was the roster of eighty brands belonging to Duke's Continental Tobacco Company; almost all were asterisked by Connorton, indicating "ownership proven and incontestable." Among the lesser-known were such names as *Admiral Dewey, American Beauties* (first used as a "fighting" or cut-priced brand), *Capt. Kidd, Columbus, Cream of Virginia, Genteel, Honey Chunk, Klondike, Royal Crown, Silk Plush, Vogue, Good Luck,* and *Old Colonial.* One was called *Horse Shoe* and another, inexplicably, *Fire Cracker.* The American Tobacco Company proper listed only a few brands; Continental was the major cigarette repository.

In the smoking tobacco department, among such weird names as *Ham Bone Granulated,* there were *Half and Half,* then made by Cameron & Cameron of Richmond, and *Lucky Strike,* made by R. A. Patterson of the same city.

Duke's corporate structure itself bore some resemblance to the catalogue of registered brand names. To preserve the valuable local reputations of subsidiary firms, many were not consolidated but kept intact as corporate entities. American Tobacco

and Continental were themselves subsidiaries after 1901, when Consolidated Tobacco was set up as a holding company, after the financial fashion of the day. Its directors, however, were no longer men like Ginter, Kinney and Kimball. They had sold out, and their places were taken by New York financial powers who had helped Duke to get expansion cash. Also represented on the board were the Union Tobacco entrepreneurs already mentioned, industrial notables like Ryan, Payne, Schley, Widener, Brady, Whitney. The character of ownership had been transformed; tycoons rather than tobaccomen were in command. Washington Duke himself no longer took an active part; like Ginter, Kinney and Kimball, he had neither the talent nor the taste for high finance. At one point the elder Duke is supposed to have confessed: "I wish Buck had never put us into the company and that we could carry on our business like we used to do it." But for Buck, there was no turning back. He too was making the transition from tobaccoman to tycoon.

By 1903 Duke's combine was in full flower. But at 83, old Wash Duke (second from left, seated) was devoted to Durham civic affairs, left the business to Buck (third from left, seated) and Ben (left).

OUT OF MANY, ONE

THE YEAR 1904 was noteworthy for two reasons. One: James B. Duke finally gathered his many tobacco manufactories into a single corporation. Two: a Williams College sophomore named George Hill quit school to work for American Tobacco at $5 a week, hauling purchased leaf from the warehouse floor at Wilson, North Carolina.

The motive for the corporate reorganization, in which American, Consolidated and Continental merged in a new American Tobacco Company, was a legal one. The U. S. Supreme Court had just declared the Northern Securities Company illegal. Like Consolidated Tobacco, Northern Securities was purely a holding company. It was set up as a settlement of the famous railroad war between James J. Hill, who controlled the Northern Pacific and Great Northern roads, and Edward H. Harriman, who controlled Union Pacific. By placing all three lines under a holding company in which the two titans shared ownership, a long and costly financial battle was ended. But since the arrangement also ended real railroad competition in the nation's northwestern quarter, the Supreme Court decided the Sherman Anti-Trust Act had been violated. The Northern Securities case broke new ground for the application of that Act.

Meanwhile, Duke kept up his growth pace, following the rules of the game as they had evolved during the nineties. The first half-dozen years of the new American Tobacco Company saw its Bright cigarette sales rise from two to more than five billion, while the more expensive Turkish brands went from 400,000,000 to 1,700,000,000. The latter figure, reached in 1910, represented a little over half the Turkish market.

Stable profits . . .

During these years profit on domestic sales was remarkably constant—a little under one mill, or one-tenth of a cent, per cigarette. (The 1953 profit was about one thirty-fifth of a cent net.) Thus in 1904 the reorganized Company showed a profit of $2.4 million on domestic sales of 2,600,000,000 cigarettes; as unit sales went to 7,100,000,000 in 1910, the cigarette profit climbed to $6.9 million. Expressed as a percentage of dollar sales, the profit margin was likewise very constant. This reflected a lack of variation both in the cost of leaf tobacco and in the price charged for packaged cigarettes.

. . . stable prices . . .

Nickel denominations were still the rule, and

Duke turned out at least one luxury item in every line, even if it yielded minimum profit. Thus in Turkish cigarettes he had Egyptienne Straights and Pall Mall Originals; in cigars, La Corona along with Bock and Cabañas; in plug, Piper Heidsieck; in smoking tobacco, Imperial Cube Cut. Significantly, all of them are still manufactured and sold today.

the law allowed packages of ten, twenty, fifty or a hundred cigarettes. The cheapest of American's brands—*Coupon, King Bee, Home Run*—sold at twenty for a nickel. The "standard brands" of the day —*Sweet Caporal* and *Piedmont*—went at ten for a nickel, as did the cheaper Turkish blends, *Mecca* and *Hassan*. The better Turkish blends sold up to 25c for ten. It was Duke's policy to set a price and stick to it if at all possible, but in 1910 taxes were raised again. Fortunately, boxes of eight and fifteen cigarettes were made legal at the same time, so the Company was able to reduce the size of the package instead of changing the price. *Coupon* and *Home Run* were then sold in boxes of fifteen to retail at the customary nickel.

. . . stable leaf . . .

Notwithstanding the off-again, on-again tax levies, Duke was lucky enough to strike a period of stable leaf costs. Then as now, tobacco itself was the major expense of manufacture, amounting to half the price to jobbers or even more, net of excise taxes. During the first thirty years of Duke's cigarette operations, Bright tobacco averaged a fairly steady 10c a pound on the Danville market, going no higher than 13c and no lower than 7c in a few exceptional years. This stability was logical enough: for one thing,

cigarette consumption was only a small part of total tobacco use; secondly, the price of leaf was determined by a really free bidding system.

. . . unstable mood

Lucky as he was in the matter of leaf prices, Duke was unlucky in the climate of his public relations. The two decades ending in 1910 was a time of bubbling unrest among the farm population. The Agricultural Revolution had not caught up with the Industrial Revolution, and the profits registered by the new big business organizations led first to envy and later to muckraking. William Jennings Bryan shouted "You shall not crucify mankind upon a cross of gold" (he would have settled for a cross of silver), and the social pangs of mechanization and urbanization were often blamed on the trusts.

During the "gay" nineties, many of which were years of economic depression, resentment against giant corporations sharpened. Antitrust suits were brought against the Duke firm in North Carolina, New Jersey, New York, Missouri, Illinois, Kentucky and Massachusetts. All were thrown out but the last, in which an overzealous Continental Tobacco salesman was convicted of restraining trade by persuading jobbers to deal only in his company's goods. Nevertheless, until the Northern Securities decision of 1904, the rules of the game seemed in no danger of being changed. In the Knight case of 1895 the Supreme Court itself refused to break up the Sugar Trust, which refined 98% of the nation's sugar. And combination was encouraged by New Jersey, Delaware, Maine and other states, whose laws specifically authorized chartered corporations to hold stock in other corporations. In 1904, the year of re-incorporation, Duke's combine made 88% of the nation's cigarettes, 80% of its quid, 75% of its smoking tobacco, over 90% of its snuff, and 14% of its cigars. It was not at all strange that old Wash Duke, now a wry and whimsical eighty-four, should have introduced himself on a European trip as the "Duke of Durham."

AT in 1906

What, exactly, made up the Dukedom? Forty years after Wash Duke made his wagon junket to Raleigh, The American Tobacco Company had a capitalization of $235 million, of which $78.7 million was in preferred stock, $40.2 million in common stock, and the rest in bonds. Of the common stock, $35.5 million was owned by fifty-two people, and the ten largest stockholders owned 63%. These included six directors—James and Benjamin Duke, Thomas Fortune Ryan, Anthony Brady, O. H. Payne and P. A. B. Widener—along with the Wall Street firm of Moore & Schley, Grant B. Schley himself, and the Whitney and Elkins estates. Among those owning $100,000 or more in common stock were Percival Hill, George Arents, R. J. Reynolds, Pierre Lorillard and R. A. Patterson, originator of the *Lucky Strike* smoking tobacco.

In turn, American Tobacco owned 66% of British-American Tobacco, 83.5% of American Cigar and 43% of American Snuff. There were also seventy-seven smaller subsidiaries, grouped as follows:

Cigarette group: S. Anargyros, John Bollman, Wells-Whitehead, and Monopol. More than half the Company's cigarettes were made in New York, at the Kinney-Duke branch on 22nd Street and in the Anargyros Turkish factory. Most of the remaining half were turned out in Richmond. The Brooklyn plant, called the Penn Street Branch, had not yet attained the volume which was to make it known as the "House of *Mecca.*" There were a scattering of lesser factories in New Orleans, Wilson (North Carolina), and San Francisco, as well as little-cigar plants in Danville, Baltimore, Philadelphia and New York.

Plug group: F. R. Penn, R. J. Reynolds, D. H. Spencer & Sons, Lipfert-Scales, Nall & Williams, Nashville Tobacco Works. Almost half the Company's plug was made in the St. Louis plant of Liggett & Myers-Drummond. Most was navy plug and twist, heavily flavored and sweetened dark Burley leaf, sold under the *Star, Horse Shoe, Big Gun, Good Luck, Natural Leaf, Burley Cable, Honey Dip* and *Oklahoma Twist* labels, among others. Second in size was another navy plug manufactory, the National Tobacco Works at Louisville. Its brand names included *American Eagle, Autumn, Battle Ax, Black Bass, Brandywine, Burr Oak, Jolly Tar, Newsboy, Tennessee Cross Tie* and the famous "champagne" brand, *Piper Heidsieck.* Third largest was the Reynolds plant at Winston, specializing in flat sweetened plug. The F. R. Penn Company, at Reidsville, North

As excise tax dropped to 1.08c per pack, five-cent cigarettes revived. Home Run was among American's many nickel brands, as were Coupon and King Bee.

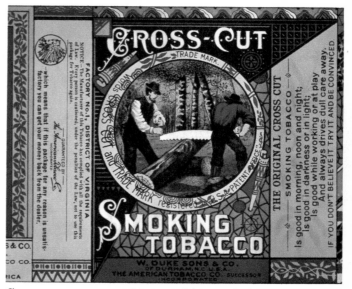

Same name was used on smoking and chewing tobacco, cigarettes, cigars, cheroots and even snuff. One such name was Crosscut, first registered in 1881.

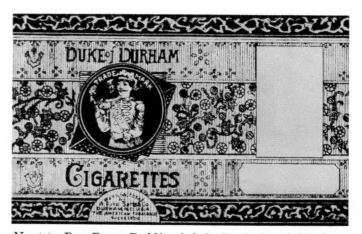

Next to Pro Bono Publico label, the Duke of Durham brand (1871) was American's oldest. In Europe, wry old Wash Duke was introduced as the Duke of Durham.

Carolina, produced a plug and a smoking tobacco under the same name—*Penn's No. 1.*

Smoking tobacco group: Blackwell's Durham, R. A. Patterson, John W. Carroll, R. P. Richardson, P. Lorillard, Spaulding & Merrick, F. F. Adams. Much of their so-called "smoking tobacco" was actually chewed. There were three kinds—granulated; long-cut, which was shredded into long strands in the manner of cigarette filler; and plug cut, which was pressed into solid slabs before shredding. The entire output of Duke-Durham and Blackwell's Durham branch—more than a quarter of the Company's output—was granulated. The other big smoking tobacco factory at Jersey City made all three types, plus "scrap," a cased (flavored) assortment of cigar cuttings. The major scrap factory was the Luhrman & Wilbern Company at Middletown, Ohio. Also classified in the scrap tobacco group: Queen City and Day and Night tobacco companies of Cincinnati, and the Pinkerton Tobacco Company of Zanesville, Ohio.

Contributory group: MacAndrews & Forbes, a licorice importer; the Mengel, Columbia and Tyler box companies; Golden Belt, a bag manufacturer; Conley and Johnston foil companies; American Machine & Foundry, New Jersey Machine, International Cigar Machinery, Standard Tobacco Stemmer and Garson Vending Machine companies; Kentucky Tobacco Products and Kentucky Tobacco Extract companies; Baltimore and Manhattan briar pipe companies; Amsterdam Supply, a purchasing subsidiary; and Thomas Cusack Company, a bill poster.

Distributing group: United Cigar Stores, comprising 392 retail outlets under four corporations, along with five other distributors.

Snuff group: W. E. Garrett, Weyman & Bro. (now evolved into the United States Tobacco Company) and Standard Snuff.

Cigar group: American Cigar, Federal Cigar,

First decade of this century was the heyday of the dealer in tobacco exclusively. Storefront sculpture throve.

Henry Clay & Bock, Cuban Land and Leaf Tobacco, H. de Cabañas y Carbajal and twenty-three other organizations of which the largest (next to American Cigar) were American Stogie, Havana-American, Havana Tobacco, Havana Cigar and Tobacco Factories, and Porto Rican-American.

In most cases, ownership in these subsidiaries amounted to 50% or more.

This rather complicated hierarchy was maintained for several reasons. First, many of the subsidiaries were really investments, which could be controlled with a majority holding at half the cost required for outright consolidation. Second, the best of these subsidiaries were going concerns with smart and interested managers like R. J. Reynolds and Pierre Lorillard. They were stronger as semi-autonomous operations, since the men who built them retained some ownership interest as an incentive. Third, there was the merchandising value of established company names: in many cases this was a subsidiary's only valuable asset.

Two-legged assets

For the historian, the growing sentiment against the trusts was perhaps the outstanding feature of the twentieth century's first decade. But for The American Tobacco Company, only one of many combinations to be broken up, these years saw the creation of assets no court could dissolve: skilled management. After Duke left American Tobacco in 1912, these two-legged assets remained; they saw the cigarette business change radically from the multi-branded merchandising melee of his reign, and they reconstituted American Tobacco as the leader in a new kind of market. George Washington Hill, most notable product of Duke's training school, later recalled his experience of 1905:

I was working in the tobacco market at

Besides wooden Pocahontases and ballplayers (opposite page), one could see a French trapper, Jenny Lind, or Punch.

South Boston, Virginia. We had one buyer there who was unique. One of my first impressions of this man was that he could recognize at the "prizery," where the tobacco is put in hogsheads, every single pile of tobacco he had previously bought, regardless of what sale it had been bought on, what price he had paid, or what time of the day he had bought it. His name was Jim Lipscomb and his knowledge of tobacco was a by-word.

I never forgot Jim Lipscomb as a buyer of tobacco, and when it came to my lot to hold a more responsible position with the Company than I did in those days, I was not satisfied until he was made our head buyer, in charge of all our purchases of tobacco.

Two years later, the Company acquired a small New York outfit called Butler-Butler, and young Hill was put in charge. Like most cigarette companies, Butler-Butler owned many brands, but Hill decided to concentrate on only one. The era of the "big brand" may be dated from that decision. His choice was a straight Turkish cigarette, *Pall Mall*. In 1940, when *Pall Mall* was getting started as a king-sized Burley blend, Hill remembered that

> . . . in Butler-Butler, there was a man named Vincent Riggio. When I took charge he had just been promoted from the sales force to the position of Division Manager. He had eight or ten men working under his supervision in and around New York City, and he was doing a fine job.

In men and in brands, the contribution of little Butler-Butler was way out of proportion to its size. In addition to Riggio, who was a barber before he was brought into the firm as a bottom-rung salesman, there was another New York lad named Edmund Harvey who had come to the Butlers in 1898 as a fourteen-year-old office boy. For forty years after George Hill took over Butler-Butler, Harvey served as his No. 1 troubleshooter. At various times he was Field Sales Manager, Credit Manager, Auditor of American Cigar, Treasurer, and is currently Vice President for sales. Brandwise, B-B brought to American two Turkish brands which for a time rivaled the domestic blends in importance—*Pall Mall* and *Egyptienne Straights*. Among the oddments were a Bright cigarette called *Sovereign*, another called *Horse Guards* and a "Frenchified" brand named *Laurens*, each box of which contained five playing cards.

The cigaret sandwich

Hill himself had undergone a rigorous traineeship. After hustling tobacco on the flue-cured markets, he followed the leaf one step further as a submanager of the Durham stemmery. For a time he manufactured Carolina Bright cigarettes at Wilson, North Carolina, then went on the road as a salesman. By the time he moved "inside" as President of Butler-Butler, he had reached the conclusion—one doubted by Duke—that cigarettes were the coming thing. Hill labored over the "gorgeous" red *Pall Mall* package, then a box, supervised magazine advertising, devised new variants of the prize-in-every-package. Many of the miniature flags and blankets he sandwiched between rows of *Sovereigns* ended as homemade scarves or pillows. At one time, *Egyptienne Straights* boxes contained short stories instead—printed tales by Rudyard Kipling, Stephen Leacock, Earl Derr Biggers or Anthony Hope in the form of little booklets, whose size—about two by three inches—guaranteed that the stories were truly "short."

It must have required a very prescient mind indeed to single out the cigarette as the star of the future. Of the 281,000,000 pounds of leaf utilized in all of the factories in 1906, less than 10,000,000 went into domestic and blended cigarettes at the three big factories in New York, Richmond and New Orleans. The Turkish factories in New York and San Fran-

In 1904 two-thirds of American Tobacco common was owned by ten men. Thomas Fortune Ryan was one of them, along with financiers Brady, Payne, Widener.

cisco accounted for 1,874,000 pounds more; Wells-Whitehead's Caroline Brights, on which George Hill cut his sales teeth, consumed 301,000 pounds. The cigarette total was only half the tobacco processed by the Duke-Durham smoking branch alone, less than a fourth of that used in the St. Louis plug plant.

Percy Hill, first lieutenant

In devoting himself almost wholly to cigarettes, young Hill doubtless encountered some paternal resistance from his father. Percival S. Hill was now one of J. B. Duke's top Vice Presidents; prior to 1904 he had been marked as one of the Company's elite by his directorship in the holding company, Consolidated Tobacco. The elder Hill, more of a traditionalist than his son, had been raised on the glories of *Bull Durham*. He had personally engaged Rosa Bonheur to create a new image of that mighty beast. And in 1898, American soldiers in Cuba and the Philippines had derived solace not only from the famous smoking tobacco but from postcards distributed by the Blackwell company—each card, naturally, bearing a pictorial reminder of its taurine trademark. By the time George Hill was getting *Pall Mall* fairly started, *Bull Durham* was acknowledged to be "the standard of the world." It was, certainly, the most widely used single tobacco product: in 1912, for example, American departed from usual policy to

publicize its sales total of 350,000,000 bags. This was enough to roll almost twelve billion cigarettes—more than the number of "white rolls" being manufactured by machine.

But George Hill had become an acute trend-reader during his drummer days. In the first two years of the new American Tobacco Company, tax-paid withdrawals of chewing tobacco were down. And although "chaw," along with smoking tobacco, later resumed its slight year-by-year increase, neither kept up with population growth. The weakening in per capita consumption of manufactured tobacco was particularly evident between 1904 and 1910, during which period the fictional "average citizen" increased his cigarette usage by 138%.

These years, however, were bringing more than a subtle change in smoking tastes. Time had run out on Washington Duke, who died in 1905. It was running out on the trust as well. In July, 1907, two months after the acquisition of Butler-Butler, the U. S. Government brought suit against The American Tobacco Company for combination in restraint of trade. The suit, begun by Trustbusting Teddy Roosevelt, did not reach its climax in the Supreme Court until November 16, 1911. At that point William Howard Taft was President of the United States; very shortly thereafter, James Buchanan Duke ceased to be President of The American Tobacco Company.

Also an owner-director was Benjamin Duke (left), J. B. Duke's older brother. Pierre Lorillard (center) and R. J. Reynolds each owned more than $100,000 of *the common stock. Combination was not illegal; in fact, the holding of one company's stock by another was encouraged by laws in New Jersey and elsewhere.*

Out of one, many

It was ironic that the man who actually dismantled the Tobacco Trust was the man who built it, J. B. Duke. In May, 1911, the Supreme Court held the combination "in restraint of trade and an attempt to monopolize and a monopolization." It provided eight months "to hear the parties . . . for the purpose of ascertaining and determining upon some plan or method of dissolving the combination . . ." The plan was prepared by Duke, approved by the Attorney General, and published as a Court decree on November 16, 1911. After this, Duke himself virtually discontinued his active participation in the day-to-day affairs of the Company, and scarcely used his office at 111 Fifth Avenue. Early in 1912 Duke left the Company to become board Chairman of British-American Tobacco, a post he held until 1923.*

The plan spun off many of the more independent subsidiaries. MacAndrews & Forbes (which had been decreed a licorice paste monopoly in 1907) was separated, along with American Snuff, Conley Foil, American Stogie, British-American Tobacco, Imperial Tobacco, United Cigar Stores, R. J. Reynolds, and Porto Rican-American Cigar. The purchasing subsidiary, Amsterdam Supply, was killed outright. American Machine & Foundry was turned loose voluntarily, since it could not legally do business with the new companies while still part of American.

The American Tobacco Company itself was pared to $98 million in asset value. Of the remaining assets, $67 and $48 million went into two new companies, Liggett & Myers and P. Lorillard. About half the book assets represented "brands and goodwill." In this most vital aspect of the dissolution, Lorillard got *Helmar, Egyptian Deities, Turkish Trophies, Murad* and *Mogul*, or about 15% of the nation's cigarette business. Liggett was given *Piedmont, American Beauty, Fatima, Home Run, Imperiales, Coupon* and *King Bee*, representing a 28% slice of the cigarette market. American retained a 37% share of the cigarette market. The rather uneven re-alignment of the cigarette business (and that of plug and smoking tobacco as well) resulted from the

---

*Duke never strayed from his emphasis on Bright tobacco, which partly accounts for the lasting popularity of "straight Virginia" blends in Britain.

assignment of whole factories to the successor companies to avoid undue "disturbance" to operations.

Distribution of the cigarette brands was not, relatively, a major feature of the asset split-up. In 1910 cigarettes contributed only 21% of the Company's operating profit. Cigarette earnings were less than those from either plug or smoking tobaccos—less than the combined profits from snuff and cigars. Not until the early 1940s would the white rolls account for more than 90% of the Company's business, as they do today.

Among the human assets lost to the Company was a young manufacturing man named Preston Fowler. Among other things Fowler had supervised

F. R. Penn, a plugmaking subsidiary, was the major industry in Reidsville, North Carolina, made Penn's Natural, Red J, Gold Crumbs. A shipment of 25,000 pounds of Gold Crumbs in 1909 rated this photograph.

the production of Turkish cigarettes and was "awarded" along with them to Lorillard. In 1930, however, Fowler "came home" to American Tobacco and is now Vice President in charge of manufacture.

The Attorney General himself, George W. Wickersham, felt the agreed division far more desirable than utter disintegration which would have led to "injury to the general business condition of the country." For his pains Wickersham was verbally tarred by the self-styled "Tar Heel Editor," Josephus Daniels, who took to printing the official's name as Wicker*sham*. It was Daniels who quoted Josh Reynolds' exuberant reaction to dissolution: "Watch me and see if I don't give Buck Duke hell."

There were cons as well as pros. The original antitrust verdict of 1908, in the U. S. Circuit Court of New York, had declared in part: "The record . . . does not indicate that there has been any increase in the price of tobacco products to the consumer. There is an absence of persuasive evidence that by unfair competition or improper practices independent dealers have been dragooned into . . . selling out . . . . . . The price of leaf tobacco . . . has steadily increased until it has nearly doubled, while at the same time 150,000 additional acres have been devoted to tobacco crops . . . new markets have been opened in India, China and elsewhere."

All of which, the majority decision went on,

Before War I Reidsville's baseballers were called "Red Js." Smiling shortstop (standing, second from left) was William Nichols, now manager of Company's Reidsville plant. Ballplayers are now the "Luckies."

was overshadowed by the new construction of the Sherman Act, as outlawing any combination in restraint of competition. Wrote one embittered journalist following the Supreme Court's confirmation of this view: "The only serious complaint against the tobacco company comes from American competitors, who have not the experience, capital, business foresight, sagacity and energy to enter the field like true warriors . . . But business success in this country does not come of childish whining."

But neither could adult carping reverse the course of legal history, and the division stood. In addition to the cigarette split-up, Lorillard and Liggett each got a fifth of the smoking tobacco business;

Liggett a third and Reynolds a fifth of the plug trade; Liggett two-fifths and Lorillard a fourth of the fine-cut smoking tobacco market; and Lorillard about half the trust's cigar business, which had amounted to about 13% of all unit sales.

To all this, the reaction of J. B. Duke himself was astonishingly unemotional. Possibly the dissolution held a personal challenge for him because J. P. Morgan thought it impractical: "You can't unscramble eggs," said the mighty banker. In any event, Duke later recalled: "I don't know that the combine was really of much advantage to us after all. We were doing well as we were; we were beating the other fellows in manufacturing and selling anyway. I believe we would, in time, have put them out of the running and gotten practically all the business if there never had been any combination."

What was the effect of the great dissolution on the consumer? It was, to begin with, surprisingly slight. In 1913 the successor companies had the same combined share of the plug, smoking, fine-cut, snuff, cigarette and cigar business as the 1910 trust – give or take a couple of percentage points. Retail prices did not change. Leaf prices varied no more than ordinary crop differences would account for. Factory costs remained constant. But one thing did change: the cost of selling. Competition among the new Big Four increased sales costs from 1910's $7.2 million to $9.8 million in 1913; advertising expenditures went from $10.9 million to $23.6 million. As a result, the Commissioner of Corporations wryly noted that "the aggregate amount of profit of the successor companies in 1913 was slightly less than that of the combination in 1910 in spite of a larger volume of sales." The profit shrinkage showed most, naturally, where the competitive scramble was keenest, *i.e.*, in domestic cigarettes. The combination's margin of 76c per thousand was cut to an average of 27c for the successor companies in 1913.

The reason for this lay in the dissolution decree itself. Instead of parceling out a selection of brands to each successor, the decree awarded Lorillard most of the 10c and 15c Turkish brands, Liggett the only 15c Turkish blend and the low-priced domestic brand names, and Reynolds nothing in the cigarette line. American kept the highest-quality Turkish brand, *Pall Mall,* along with the domestic

Duke was in his prime when dissolution was ruled. In fact, he was almost the only man who knew enough about the business to "unscramble the tobacco egg."

George W. Wickersham, U. S. Attorney General, made up the plan of division with Duke. He was against disintegration lest it harm the country's economy.

Sweet Caporal and *Hassan* and *Mecca* in the low-priced Turkish field. Elements of confusion were not lacking: *Cameo* as a cigarette was awarded to Liggett & Myers, while *Cameo* as a smoking tobacco—with a label almost identical—was retained by American.

Each company struck out at once to plug the gaps in its cigarette line. American brought out *Omar*, a high-grade Turkish blend. Liggett tried a Turkish item called *Vafiadis* and tested a new domestic cigarette under the old name of *Chesterfield*. Lorillard made *Zira* and *Nebo* to fight *Mecca* and *Hassan*. Reynolds tried *Reyno* in the nickel class and *Osman* in the 15c category. Most of this experimentation, it will be seen, was directed at the growing taste for Turkish names and atmosphere, if not Turkish tobacco in straight form. It was to evolve something quite non-Oriental, however, in everything but name.

In 1907, the jackbooted Josh Reynolds had devised a new granulated plug cut smoking tobacco named *Prince Albert*. The mixture contained a large dose of strong, heavily-flavored Burley leaf and appealed immediately to the rustic trade. By 1913,

P. A. was an established and successful smoking brand and Reynolds, disappointed at the nation's indifference to *Reyno* and *Osman* cigarettes, decided to adapt the *Prince Albert* formula to the white roll market. Although the result was a blend as far from Turkish as Kentucky itself, he gave it an Oriental name—*Camel*—and festooned the package with pyramids and minarets. And, mindful of the source of *Prince Albert's* growth, he introduced the new cigarette outside the big-city markets. Like *Reyno* and *Osman*, the new brand, which became known to the trade as "The Hump," was intended as a down payment on the hell Reynolds had promised to give Buck Duke. Had Duke remained with American, he might have acknowledged it with thanks. For *Camel* touched off an advertising and promotional rivalry which swept both Turkish and straight Bright cigarettes into the background and began the era of the big brands, the blended brands, the standard brands. The industry was to achieve mass production of a kind Duke never dreamed of in the chaotic no-brand's-land of 1900.

ASK DAD, HE KNOWS

IT IS TRUE enough that George Washington Hill, as a brash young man of twenty-five, began the "big brand" era in cigarettes. He was responsible for Butler-Butler's concentration on *Pall Mall*, a concentration at wide variance with the old pattern, the crowded battlefield of brands. He followed the hallowed custom of premium lures developed by Major Lewis Ginter and J. B. Duke, but started something of his own by advertising *Pall Mall* on back covers of magazines ("A Shilling in London, A Quarter Here"). Later he dog-fought Josh Reynolds on a broad, bold scale which led to national advertising and real mass production.

But to do any of this, he had to ask his dad. And his dad knew the answers. Percival S. Hill was named President of American Tobacco by the departing Buck Duke, and held that office for fourteen years until his death in 1925. He was a quiet, moderate man who had been devoted to Duke. He had learned the smoking tobacco business as the handler of *Bull Durham*, and had been given charge of the trust's cigarette business by J. B. More important, he had absorbed Duke's theory of handling men, of getting the best out of his managers. As we have seen, the major reason for Duke's policy of partial rather than complete ownership of subsidiaries was psycho-

logical: he wanted his properties run "by men who had a stake in them." And within his own executive family, Duke was a delegator; "What do you think of it?" was his favorite phrase, put to his executives before every major decision. Duke himself outlined Article XII of the Company's by-laws, providing that 10% of the profits in excess of the 1910 figure be paid out as bonuses to the President and five Vice Presidents. (On a greatly reduced scale of payments, the by-law is still in effect.)

The delegator

Percy Hill extended the Duke theory of individual responsibility all the way down the line. While he concerned himself with the Corporation's finances and with what are called "broad policies," he left the tactical decisions to subordinates and let them alone as long as they got results. John Crowe, now one of the top six officers, remembers his first man-to-man encounter with P. S. Hill. After a few years in the Louisville plug plant, he had been brought to New York as a kind of trainee-assistant to the manufacturing chief, Charles Penn, and his first lieutenant, Charles Neiley. One day while the two top men were on a factory tour, Crowe was called into an important conference in Hill's office. A special promotion on

After 1911 Duke left American Tobacco and Percival Hill became President. Hill had come up as a Bull Durham salesman to become Duke's right-hand man.

Manufacturing chief was Charles Penn, son of the Reidsville plugmaker Duke had bought out. Bred in the trade, Penn had an uncanny knowledge of leaf.

Tuxedo smoking tobacco was being worked out, and Crowe was asked whether he could get several carloads of the brand to the West Coast within a week. "I hadn't the slightest idea whether it was possible," recalls Crowe, "and besides I was scared stiff. Whatever I said, it was certainly no answer." Later on Hill called the young trainee back to his office for a private conversation: "Crowe, this business is mostly horse sense. If you don't know, say so. But your job is to get so that you do know." It was Hill's way of putting the young manufacturing man on his own, and it succeeded.

Mr. Penn of Carolina

Like the other executives George Hill was given a fairly free reign over his own domain, sales promotion. But his dad knew what things George didn't know. One of them was manufacturing, and in this department Charlie Penn's word was, by Percy Hill's own edict, law. On several occasions Penn had to stand up against the youthful Sales Vice President's bright ideas, which were generated out of a scant year's experience making Carolina Brights. And Penn did just that quite successfully in his gruff, unshakeable way.

For Penn, even more than George Washington Hill, had been bred with tobacco. His grandfather was Thomas Jefferson Penn, a direct descendant of Thomas Jefferson and William Penn. His father was the well-known F. R. Penn, whose Reidsville plug business, founded in 1838, was bought out by Buck Duke. *Penn's No. 1* and later *Penn's Natural Leaf* (still made by American Tobacco) achieved wide acceptance as a unique product — Burley filler wrapped in flue-cured leaf. The town of Reidsville itself (now centered around the production of *Lucky Strike* cigarettes) was also unique. It was a typical Southern town, as suggested by some of Penn's lesser brands — *Kitty May, Rebel Girl, Famous Friend, Dew Drop, Little Pearl, Little Daisy, Native, Old Virginia Chew.* But even more than Durham, Reidsville had been put on the map by tobacco and tobacco alone. As a manufacturing man with a knack of maintaining consistent quality control and an uncanny knowledge of leaf, Charlie Penn was also unique.

It is a peculiar fact of the tobacco business that the manufacturing side wages a continual defensive while the selling side is constantly on the go, constantly changing, constantly on the offense. For the basic requirement of sales success—quality of product—is always being threatened. Any one of a number of factors—variations in the nicotine or acid or ammonia content of each year's leaf crop, shortages in flavoring materials, shifts in the factory forces—can, if permitted, disturb the character of a cigarette blend, a smoking mixture or a twist. It was Penn's job, and later Charles Neiley's job, to defend the organization's products and processes against such influences. As sales mounted, the task became more difficult and at present, two of the five Vice Presidents handle it: Preston Fowler and John Crowe.

Selling bee

Selling, of course, is a different matter. Getting through to the public was, and is, a problem of sensing the public mood, tuning in on its precise wavelength, sounding the right note. And here Hill did for cigarettes what P. T. Barnum had done for Jenny Lind: he made them live in the public consciousness.

How?

The best clue to George Hill's early thinking is contained in a loose-leaf "diagram book" sketching his strategy for each brand. Under *"Sovereign,"* Hill wrote:

> The *Sovereign* cigarette is made of the finest Virginia and Carolina stock . . . by reason of their Southern birth and tradition, the people of the territory in which *Sovereign* cigarettes are to be advertised . . . have very strong and fixed ideas of the value of family ties . . . if we may impress these people with some thought that will convey the idea that *Sovereign* cigarette is a product of genuine blood heritage and smacks of the best breeding of the Southland . . . we shall have something . . . Hence our idea for popularizing *Sovereign* must be something that will leave this impression of good will toward what we may call a "gentlemanly brand."

> Based on the foregoing, we propose to . . . humanize the cigarette; that is, make it speak in the first person as a human being and tell its own story. Having created a *Sovereign* "character" we shall have him speak as a young Southern gentleman should speak, and treat of each detail in his life in the plain, homely, colloquial terms of his section.

The heart of the plan and the selling argument is to be expressed as follows:

The expensive Pall Mall in 1912 was "a shilling in London, a quarter here." By 1919 the price was 30c. In those years it was a straight Turkish cigarette.

Pall Mall is the London street where English once played croquet, which Italians called palla-maglio, the French pale maile, and the British pall mall.

5 cts.

After 1912, George Hill was advertising strategist. Mecca combined "flavor of Turkish with character of American." Sweet Caporal, an 1868 Kinney brand, was given the nostalgic line: "Ask dad, he knows."

Sovereign cigarettes for the gentlemen of the South—the king of them all. We folks of the South know good blood. We folks of the South know good tobacco. And *Sovereign* cigarettes come from the very best stock of Virginia and the Carolinas. They are made in one of the finest, cleanest, whitest homes in all the fair Southland at Durham, N. C.

The new "print media" advertising did not take hold all at once. Inserts remained: " . . . for *twenty* SOVEREIGN coupons, packed only in SOVEREIGN 5c Packages, we will send 10 Rugs, or SOVEREIGN Coupons are redeemable for ½ cent cash." In 1912 *Mecca* postcards, lacking stamps but otherwise eminently suited for the U. S. mail, could be had for the asking at any United Cigar Store. By 1914, the cigarette sandwich began to disappear, and the premium department announced in four languages: "We will continue to pack HASSAN blankets for a short time only, as many of our consumers advise us that they have accumulated a sufficient supply of these Flag Blankets. We will then pack a Valuable HASSAN Coupon which we will redeem for useful presents of unusual value." The presents: shaving sticks, talcum powder, razors, shears, knives, clocks and, naturally, cigarette cases. Premium lures were ceasing to satisfy by the beginning of War I, and after 1920 they were not a major factor in the sales of any important brands. The sales argument, the "reason why" became more potent than prizes.

Hill's formula was to find an attribute in each product that could be conveyed in vivid, impressionistic terms. In a 1916 memo to his advertising manager, he groped for a *Sweet Caporal* theme:

> Mention the name *Sweet Caporal* to almost any man you meet and his reply, with some interesting tale of his younger days will be: "*Sweet Caps* was my first smoke and it was good too."
> To the millions of men who found in their first smoke solace, comfort and joy in *Sweet Caps*, the very name brings back to their memories the romance, the interesting events, the struggles and yes, the frivolities of their younger days.
> Therefore, our plan is based on the reminiscent appeal to Dad's generation and the romantic memories of it by the present generation. The heart of this plan and the selling argument is to be expressed as follows:
> *Sweet Caporals* are dad's cigarettes because

Low-priced Turkish cigarettes did well until after War I. Lord Salisbury, American's entry, was "the only 100% pure, all-Turkish cigarette in the world that sells for as little money as 15c for twenty."

they're the purest way to smoke tobacco. *Sweet Caps* certainly stood the test of forty years because more are sold today than ever. They must be pure and mild and good or they would have been forgotten long ago—like Mother's pie, they simply can't be improved on. Ask dad, he knows.

Hill pored over every cigarette and tobacco brand, developing his aptitude for combining strong logic with picturesque language. The *Lord Salisbury* brand had this selling argument: " . . . the only 100% pure, all-Turkish tobacco cigarette in the world that sells for as little money as 15c for Twenty, *Twenty*, TWENTY Cigarettes." Hill's thoughts on the *Mecca* blend were subsumed under the heading, TO ALL PEOPLE MECCA MEANS GOAL:

> When Turkish tobacco was brought to this country, smokers thought for a time they had found the cigarette they had been looking for. But they soon found that Turkish tobacco lacked something. It had flavor, but it lacked character. On the other hand, straight American tobacco didn't have quite the flavor smokers wanted. The *Mecca* blend solved the question. *Mecca* . . . combined the flavor of Turkish tobacco with the character of American. So *Mecca* became "the blend men were looking for—a real man's smoke—the goal of all cigarette smokers."

Hill's efforts, like those of all creators, were variable. The "logical premise" for *Omar*, the Turkish and domestic blend, was:

> OMAR OMAR spells Aroma (salesman should here take his pencil and illustrate the trick). *Omar* is Aroma—Rich and Ripe Aroma. Aroma makes a cigarette; they've told you that for years. Smoke *Omar* for Aroma.

Despite his passion for the cigarette, young Hill did not neglect the smoking tobaccos which were still the backbone of American's business. *Bull Durham's* slogan, "The Makings of a Nation," was elaborated via this copy:

> *You* can make for yourself, with your own hands, the mildest, most fragrant cigarette in the world—and the most economical. Machines can't imitate it. The only way to get that freshness, that flavor, that lasting satisfaction

Once a prime attraction, miniature rugs and flags were on the way out by War I. Hassan smokers, who "advise us that they have accumulated a sufficient supply of Flag Blankets" were given notice in four languages that the old inserts would give way to a coupon redeemable for clocks, razors, knives, etc.

Omar, added to the older Mecca and Hassan among the Turkish-domestic blends, soon outstripped either: during War I, most Omars went overseas to soldiers.

is to "roll your own" with good old 'Bull' Durham tobacco.

Sugar for the Bull

Despite this appeal, the tailor-made cigarette was clearly displacing the hand-rolled variety. Hill recognized this by inventing a second theme for the aging Bull, "Like Sugar in Your Coffee." This was a suggestion to pipe smokers to "just try mixing a little genuine *Bull Durham* tobacco with your favorite pipe tobacco." As Hill explained it to his advertising man, "The distinct, mellow-sweet taste, which is so individual a factor of *Bull Durham*, does give just that added touch to pipe tobacco that sugar gives to coffee."

Chocolate for Tuxedo

One of Hill's favorite copy subjects was *Tuxedo* smoking tobacco. Like any Burley blend, the leaf was heavily flavored (unlike Bright tobacco, the Burley leaf contains no natural sugar). But instead of using only rum or juices, the normal Burley casing, *Tuxedo*'s formula also called for chocolate. "We find by actual test," memo'd Hill, "that *Tuxedo*, when rubbed in the palm of the hand until the heat generates and brings out its full odor, compares very favorably and indeed, is superior in flavor and fragrance to other tobaccos to which this same test is applied. This point and thought is, we believe, expressed clearly in the sentence, 'Your Nose Knows' and it is this thought that we propose to develop.

"The reason for this difference is fundamental —*Tuxedo* is flavored with chocolate and not with rum; other granulated Burleys are flavored with rum . . . The comparison is therefore very strong. The knowledge of this comparison and of *Tuxedo*'s superior flavor and fragrance will, we believe, increase the sales . . . " The actual slogan used to promote *Tuxedo* was "Your Nose Knows"; but this is less interesting than that part of the copy which read: "Rub a little *Tuxedo* briskly in the palm of your hand to bring out its aroma." This was the germ of the demonstration idea, later to blossom in Hill's fertile mind with surprising results.

Shakedown cruise

The experimentation of the post-dissolution years was not confined to advertising. For the first ten years of Percy Hill's presidency, both the sales and manufacturing departments were on a kind of shakedown cruise. Not until 1923 did the corporate organization settle into a shape approximating its present one.

At first, George Hill split his sales force into divisions which competed with one another, like the divisions of today's General Motors Corporation. Vincent Riggio and R. L. Armstrong had the Butler brands; there was a *Mecca* division, a *Hassan* division, a tobacco brands department, and a general sales department which embraced plug. Tying the cigarette business together was a cigarette committee, of which Edmund Harvey was secretary.

Decentralization, to be sure, had worked before—Reynolds had built up a respectable smoking tobacco trade and enlarged its plug business in competition with other arms of the trust, and its success with the new *Camel* may have further impressed the Hills with the virtues of small, self-contained units free to act independently. But in practise, the theory didn't hold. Atomization of the sales effort produced competition, but it also led to wasteful duplication and even to personal friction between division chiefs. Besides, as Hill testified twenty-five years later, "We had plenty of competition from the outside." Eventually, the sales group was recentralized. Harvey was sent on a four months' tour of the U. S. to map out

Tuxedo tobacco was a favorite of George Hill's, for its chocolate flavoring lent itself to interesting advertising, led to the tag line "Your Nose Knows." Along with these media ads, prize coupons continued.

National distribution made the era of big brands possible. American's salesmen got exact routes to follow as well as Model T Fords to follow them in.

Salesmen did more than unload goods. They saw that stale stock did not remain on retail counters and aided sales with point-of-purchase display cards.

Edmund A. Harvey, who began with Butler-Butler, was G. W. Hill's troubleshooter from the first. He served in treasury, credit and sales, is now Vice President.

salesmen's routes. There was no precedent to guide him; the scientific consumer survey and the sales map bristling with pins had not yet appeared in the nation's head offices. Distribution, now as important as manufacture itself, was in its infancy. "What we did for ourselves," recalls Harvey, "we did for the industry."

New sights for sales

Among other things, Hill and Harvey pulled their salesmen off the milk runs and outfitted them with Model T Fords. Just as this was accomplished, Percy Hill called Harvey in to discuss another problem. "We're losing $1.2 million a year on damaged goods. That's too much." Harvey got to work, revamped selling policy. The answers he came up with were soon a part of standard operating procedure, not only for American Tobacco but for the industry.

The first item was the use of the sales force to monitor distribution, to see that jobbers moved the old stock first. This was implemented by a modification of refund policy—after six months, old goods could not be returned at 100% of the purchase price. Goods were dated to facilitate quick checkups, as is still done. A beginning in the art of fresh-packaging was made with *Penn's Natural Leaf* plug, which was vacuum-packed. (Cellophane, along with the other wonders of the Plastic Age, was still a long way off.)

New sites for manufacturing

On the manufacturing side, cigarette activities were concentrated in New York. There was the old Kinney-Duke branch on 22nd Street, turning out *Sweet Caporal, Mecca* and *Hassan;* the Butler-Butler branch a few blocks uptown, producing *Pall Mall* and *Egyptienne Straights.* There was a miscellany of brands made at the old Penn Street branch in Brooklyn, later moved to that borough's Park Avenue. The National Tobacco Works Branch at Louisville was devoted entirely to plug: *Battle Ax,* the old fighting brand; *Piper Heidsieck,* the "gentleman's quid," still a big seller; and *Black Eagle,* made of sun-cured tobacco. *Red J* and, of course, *Penn's Natural Leaf* were still made in Reidsville, N. C.

In 1916, George Hill's whole-souled devotion to *Pall Mall* must have seemed like a mistake. Although the "Famous Cigarettes" were far and away

Packaging began to be modernized under Percy Hill. Penn's Natural plug was vacuum-packed. Cigarettes like Omar were wrapped, above, in "cup packages" in lieu of boxes, hard to handle and slow to fill.

the leader in their price class, there was as yet no volume market for a 25c product. Furthermore, the fancy for Turkish straights and even Turkish blends was dissolving. *Fatima*, Liggett's Turkish blend, was being thrust into limbo by the fast-rising Burley-blended *Camel*, and the two big Bright blends—American's *Sweet Caporal* and Liggett's *Piedmont*—were likewise beginning to be superseded. The answer to this situation was *Lucky Strike*.

Enter Lucky Strike

The name was taken from an old smoking tobacco, made in Richmond for many years by R. A. Patterson, who first registered the brand in May of 1871. The Burley blend, which competed with that of the new *Camel* cigarette, was devised by Charlie Penn in the Brooklyn factory. George Hill worked with artists to eliminate the curlicues from the old trademark, and puzzled over means to sell the new cigarette under it.

Oddly enough, George Hill finally concluded he didn't want to put the new creation on the market;

as chief of sales, he would have been responsible if it failed. James B. Duke, still a good friend of the management, sided with young George in a friendly way; American, he thought, had plenty of brands already. But Riggio, in the front lines of the struggle for sales, demanded something to pit against *Camel*, and this convinced Percy Hill. Told to bring it out, G. W. wandered over to the Brooklyn factory. Three blocks away, he inhaled the rich aroma of tobacco passing through the machines and this stimulated his promotional instincts.

Back at 111 Fifth Avenue, he remarked to his father: "You know there is something in that process of Charlie Penn, and I cannot express it . . . he cooks it, cooks the tobacco." The elder Hill was unimpressed: "That doesn't mean anything, he cooks the tobacco. That doesn't leave any appetizing thought particularly." At this point a cigar man, Gerson Brown, entered the room in time to catch a question from Percy Hill: "Gerson, what do you have that is appetizing to which heat is applied?" Brown immediately mentioned his morning toast, and the elder

53

The rise of cup-packaged Omar was interrupted not only by War I—which ended the Turkish fad—but by a trend toward Burley blends like Lucky Strike. First ad for Lucky Strike was simple layout below, which broke in 1917. Designed for newspapers, it emphasized taste with its fork and piece of toast.

Hill lit on the happy phrase: "That is it—it is toasted."

Burley in the bulk

There was, of course, a good deal more to launching the new brand than coining a slogan. The distinguishing ingredient of *Lucky Strike* was its generous proportion of Burley leaf, dipped in flavoring essence and "bulked" or allowed to stand in great piles for twenty-four hours or more while the tobacco absorbed the added flavors. But there were no dipping or bulking facilities in New York, and the Burley was first treated in Richmond and shipped to the Kinney-Duke Branch in New York to be blended with other tobaccos (Bright, Maryland, Turkish) and made into cigarettes. Within a year, as the new blend caught on, this makeshift had to be changed, and Brooklyn became the center of production.

"It's Toasted"

What made the brand catch on? There were as many answers as George Washington Hill had ideas. The basic reason, probably, was the public's whetted taste for Burley tobacco. An estimated 35,000,000,000 cigarettes were rolled by hand from Burley mixtures in 1916, a year in which only 21,000,000,000 ready-made cigarettes were sold. American Tobacco had been experimenting for five years to develop a satisfactory Burley cigarette, but as a Hill memorandum explained, "It was a problem . . . to discover some method of handling Burley tobacco so that it could be used in a cigarette that would remain in good condition for a reasonable length of time. This has been accomplished by the application of a new principle in cigarette making. Under this new principle the Burley tobacco is toasted. This . . . held the Burley flavor in cigarette form. The result is *Lucky Strike*, the real Burley cigarette. It is based on the original *Lucky Strike* formula.

"This new principle can for advertising purposes be compared to the toasting of bread—'like toast, buttered hot.' The technical and chemical details of what takes place in the toasting need not be explained in advertising. They would not attract the public as much as this simple suggestion of the familiar, homely toasting fork, which everyone has seen used over the kitchen stove."

The main thrust of advertising was not applied to the new cigarette until January, 1917, when the slice of toast on a fork appeared in hundreds of newspapers and billboards—always, by Hill's order, in "brutal black." In later months Hill composed several variations on the cooking theme. Steak, broiled and buttered, was used as well as toast. After the U. S. entered the World War, and Herbert Hoover's Food Administration began to promote the potato, that tuber (closely related to *Nicotiana tabacum*) found its way into *Lucky Strike* ads: " . . . what cooking does for raw potatoes it does for 'raw' tobacco—gives flavor."

Having translated the technical details into popular language, Hill was still unsatisfied. He wanted to get across the long effort American had made to come up with a top-flight Burley-blended product. Extra advertisements and throwaways were made up to tell the story behind the toasting, in the words of Hill's own memorandum.

With Riggio's sales missionaries telling the toasting story all over the country, the introduction of *Lucky Strike*, beginning in Buffalo, was a walloping success. By May of 1917, Vice President Charles Penn contracted for construction of a factory in Reidsville, to make *Luckies* exclusively. Within eighteen months, sales of the new brand were pushing 6,000,000,000—then representing about 11% of all cigarette sales. But in the last half of 1918, its share of the market inched downward, month by month, to finish the year at a mere 6%. What happened?

For one thing, *Lucky Strike*'s genius had gone to war, as its green pack was to do twenty-five years later. Hill first went overseas as a Red Cross major. Having heard shots fired in anger on three fronts without returning the compliments personally, he came back disgusted at his non-combat role. He persuaded the Army to give him a commission, went to Washington to systematize the Motor Transport Corps, was scheduled to sail for Europe on November 14, 1918. By then, of course, the big show was over and he shed his khaki.

"tobacco as much as bullets"

For another, the war itself turned the spotlight on established brands and temporarily arrested the promotion of new ones. This was no slur on the

In France, Black Jack Pershing called for "tobacco as much as bullets" to win the war. In New York, the "Our Boys in France Tobacco Fund" spared no horses in answering General Pershing's request.

The Democracy of "The Makings"

ENVIRONMENT doesn't make a man—or a "Bull" Durham smoker. There are red-blooded, self-reliant, energetic *men* in every walk of life—and these are the *millions* of men, of *all* classes and occupations, who find thorough *satisfaction* in the *fresh,* fragrant cigarettes they *roll for themselves* from "Bull" Durham tobacco.

The rugged millionaire sportsman and his able-bodied guide in the great North woods are at opposite ends of the false social scale; but in the true *measure of manhood* they meet on an *equal footing*—share the same sack of "Bull," and *respect* each other for being *men.*

GENUINE
"BULL" DURHAM
SMOKING TOBACCO
(Enough for forty hand-made cigarettes in each 5c sack)

"Bull" Durham is a *distinctive form* of tobacco enjoyment that gives *lasting satisfaction* to *more millions* of men than all other high-grade smoking tobaccos together. Approximately 12 BILLION CIGARETTES are rolled from "Bull" Durham in a year—as many as *all* brands of ready-made cigarettes in this country *combined*—and the sales are *still growing.*

Ask for FREE book of "papers" with each 5c sack

The *delightfully smooth flavor* and *rich, fresh fragrance* of "Bull" Durham hand-made cigarettes are a *revelation.* Commence today to "Roll your own."

THE AMERICAN TOBACCO COMPANY

In 1914, Bull Durham ad stressed democracy of tobacco.

"tailor-made" cigarette, whose per capita consumption had tripled since 1911. But new brands were hardly appropriate to send overseas in response to Black Jack Pershing's ringing appeal: "You ask me what we need to win this war. I answer tobacco as much as bullets." In the spring of 1918 the U. S. contracted for the entire output of *Bull Durham,* and the old brand became "the makin's of a nation" in a double sense. The government also bought up some of the *Omar* output, but when the doughboys got back the Turkish vogue had all but disappeared. During the war, Oriental leaf had become scarce and expensive, while the trend toward homegrown tobacco was accelerated not only by new brands like *Lucky Strike* and *Camel* but by the great drive to send the makin's—*i.e., Bull Durham*—to the boys in the trenches. After the Armistice, Turkish leaf continued to be hard to get, and the halcyon days of *Mecca, Hassan* and *Omar* ended by default.

The demonstrative sell

Partly for this reason, Hill gave his oldest domestic brand a last fling. *Sweet Caporal* was pushed hard alongside *Lucky* with the tag line, "Ask Dad, *He* Knows." Dad may have known, but he shared with younger men a liking for the new Burley blends. Hill stuck to his guns for several years, however, and it was *Sweet Caporal* that furnished the first example of selling by demonstration. "Ed," Hill told Harvey one day in 1923, "I've got a new idea." The paper used in *Sweet Caps* had been changed so as to yield a fine white ash instead of the sooty black residue which standard cigarette paper then gave. Hill's idea was to take some of the paper right to the public and show them how freely it burned.

Sweet Cap's chief rival, *Piedmont,* was selling well at that time on the New York waterfront, so the

In the spring of 1918 the U. S. contracted for the entire Bull Durham output to be shipped to the doughboys.

West Side pier area was chosen as the testing ground. Harvey picked out a six-foot salesman, a big wooden table and a roll of the new paper. Although they were not allowed to take their gear on the 23rd Street trolley and were even threatened with arrest, the two finally set up the table in front of a store and went into their pitch. Unfortunately, those who stopped to watch the new paper burn to a white ash were loafers rather than buyers. Then school got out, and an uninhibited urchin grabbed the change Harvey had left casually on the table. In the excitement the table was knocked over, the six-foot salesman quit and Harvey, bereft of his ammunition, retreated. Although the demonstration was standardized with a smaller table and had some success outside factories (where one could find men with jobs and change of their own), the "selling principle of demonstration" was to be reserved for *Lucky Strike* in the future.

The big brand arrives

But 1923 was a pivotal year for American Tobacco in spite of *Sweet Caporal*'s decline. Percy Hill was now in his 61st year, a dignified gentleman whose steel-trap memory for figures concealed a softening heart. Although the first rule of keeping a tobacco business solvent is to limit credit, the elder Hill, loth to crack down on one hard-pressed jobber, asked an executive to "see if he could do something for him." By now advertising was his son's great specialty—and with the big Burley blends coming on with a rush, advertising was the spearhead of the business. Ready-made cigarettes were "it." Harvey was sent to dispose of the Manhattan Briar Company, for which a cer-

1917 ad recorded demand for Bull Durham in the services.

tificate of dissolution was filed in January, 1923. At the same time the Tobacco Products Corporation, an independent manufacturer associated with the Whelan and Schulte stores, sold its plants and rented its

Whole trainloads of muslin bags left Durham for the ports. Each bag had makin's of thirty-three cigarettes.

brand names to American. Among the latter were *Herbert Tareyton* and *Melachrino*. The same year manufacturing was centralized under Charlie Penn. Reidsville, where Penn's father had made the family's products and reputation, was transformed into "Lucky Strike Town" (the Company's plant there has also made *Pall Mall* since mid-1954).

Not only on land but also in the air was there evidence of the big push behind *Lucky Strike*. The Company turned to skywriting as a new advertising medium, and during 1923 people in 122 cities from Jersey City to San Francisco craned their necks to see "Lucky Strike" spelled out at 10,000 feet. Since aerial chirography had only been invented the year before by Major J. C. Savage of the RAF, the message received rapt attention from the nation's groundlings. They could hardly fail to notice it, since the "L" alone was a mile in length. Advertising, and American Tobacco, had changed quite a bit in ten years.

End of an order

Actually, the company had been undergoing two transformations at once. It was making the changeover from the prewar emphasis on manufactured tobacco to the postwar cigarette race; and the war's aftermath had suddenly rendered its broad line of cigarette brands obsolete. By 1925, the day of the one big brand had arrived: American Tobacco sold 17,400,000,000 cigarettes of which 13,000,000,000 were *Lucky Strikes*. And the competition was even more dependent on cigarettes. Reynolds sold more than 34,000,000,000 *Camels*, Liggett & Myers over 20,000,000,000 *Chesterfields*. These three commanded 82% of the entire domestic cigarette market, and were to command even more.

Toward the close of the year, the old order ended. In October James Buchanan Duke died, and in December his old lieutenant, Percival Smith Hill, followed him. It was no longer possible to ask dad.

After 1918, the old assortment of cigarettes gave way to one big brand, Lucky Strike. Pipe tobacco and "chaw" gave way to the "tailor-made" cigarette. American's major effort centered around Luckies, *and Reidsville, North Carolina, became known as "Lucky Strike Town." In 1923 people of 122 cities including these citizens near New York's City Hall watched skywriters spell out Lucky Strike in smoke.*

"WHAT THIS COUNTRY NEEDS..."

THE YEAR 1925 also saw the passing of a man who is more famous for a chance remark than for having been Vice President of the United States. The man was Thomas R. Marshall, an Indiana Democrat who was Woodrow Wilson's running mate in 1912 and presided over the Senate during World War I. The remark was made on the rostrum of the Senate after a Republican Senator had orated grandly and at length about the nation's needs. "What this country needs," whispered Marshall to a secretary, "is a really good five cent cigar!"

Marshall's deathless phrase is, at today's price level, a contradiction in itself. A really fine cigar is the aristocrat of smoking, no more subject to nickel production than fine vintage wine. Like the best grapes, the best cigar tobacco grows only in certain areas where sun, soil and water are just right. Top leaf comes from a tiny corner of Cuba, Pinar del Rio Province in the Vuelta Abajo area, and it takes far more than a nickel's worth to make a single fine cigar.

The spell of Spain

Since Cuba was a Spanish possession until 1898, it was natural that cigar smoking should first take hold in Spain. Connecticut Valley farmers were producing cigar leaf in Revolutionary days, to be sure, but most of their crop was for export. During the build-up of American flag shipping that began with the War of 1812, a homemade cigar industry sprang up in the Nutmeg State. The products were more like stogies than real cigars: the limited leaf supply prevented much blending, and they must have burned like powder fuses. Sailors and laborers formed a market; taverns used them as giveaways and itinerant peddlers are supposed to have carried them in their wagons.

But Americans only encountered "really good cigars" when they met Spaniards. General Putnam brought some back from Havana after his 1762 expedition, and importers of Cuban sugar in the eastern seaports followed his lead. The cigar carried the exotic appeal of distant, tropical places, and its rise paralleled the rise of the clipper ships—just as the carving of ship figureheads and cigar store Indians was accomplished in the same era and by the same craftsmen. A rather exclusive clientele developed in the East, and since mass traditionally follows class, "Spanish" became a popular adjective for advertisers of tobacco. (Even John Green's original *Bull Durham* started out as *Best Flavored Spanish Smoking Tobacco*.)

By 1840 or so, cigar-rolling was a sizable industry along the Atlantic seaboard, where immi-

Cigar demand grew slowly before the war with Mexico made brown rolls fashionable. By 1859, many of the Boston Common "smoking circle" puffed fine cigars.

Seldom seen sans cigar was Ulysses S. Grant. After the battle of Lookout Mountain in Tennessee (1863) Grant and cigar were photographed on the heights.

Notable cigar fancier around 1900 was J. P. Morgan, who did not like photographers. Morgan's cigars— eight-inch Kohinoors—were made by the Company.

grant labor was plentiful. After the Mexican War, the cigar became more or less nationalized. The cigar actually preceded the pipe as a badge of the "college man," for elder-aping sophomores took to the brown roll around this time, no doubt stimulated by the example of troopers returned from Mexico.

Brown Decades, brown rolls

Because the good cigar is, in the nature of things, expensive and because it is best smoked slowly, it was a perfect after-dinner adornment for the gentleman in the drawing room. As the country began industrializing after the War Between the States and prosperity became something to be displayed as much as enjoyed, the expensive cigar flourished. It was a symbol of the Gilded Age: cigar bands matched the gingerbread woodcarving of the postbellum veranda in their ornate tracery. Big-city shops began turning out cigars made entirely of imported Havana leaf. By the time of the gay nineties, well over half of every dollar spent on tobacco went for cigars. And it was no wonder that J. B. Duke went for cigars too: they represented *the* quality product of the tobacco industry, and they seemed to promise the most growth as well as the most gross.

In these respects, Duke was correct. But after the American Cigar Company was formed in 1901, he discovered that his method, the method of volume production and mass distribution, was not appropriate to cigars. It was true then, as it is true now of the clear Havana product, that hand labor was as important as fine leaf—not so much in final rolling, now largely mechanized, but in sorting, stripping and casing the Cuban tobacco. There was thus little advantage to be gained by great capital investment. Most cigars, like most early Turkish cigarettes, were rolled by hand in small shops or in tenements on a piecework basis. Smaller and less scrupulous manufacturers took advantage of poor immigrant folk to widen their profit margins; indeed, the rise of the American Federation of Labor traces to the segar shops in which Samuel Gompers was employed before the century's turn.

Cuba

Duke's far-ranging search for the best led him inevitably to the Pearl of the Antilles, where he added the finest factories to his long list of investments. Among these were the Havana Cigar and Tobacco Factories, Ltd. which owned the *La Corona* brand originated in 1845 by Alvarez Lopez. In 1902 American Cigar organized the Cuban Land and Leaf Tobacco Company, which still owns, leases and cultivates more of the choice Vuelta Abajo tobaccoland than all other cigar companies combined. The fine old names also included *Henry Clay, Bock, La Vencedora, H. de Cabañas y Carbajal* and *Villar y Villar*. It was in a Company factory in Cuba that J. P. Morgan the elder found the right cigar for himself—a mighty roll eight inches long. (This shape, the Kohinoor, cost $1.25 apiece and was ordered by Morgan in batches of 9,000. J. P. Morgan the younger preferred a smaller cigar from the same factory, called "J.P.M.") Another financial family, the house of Rothschild, got its cigars from the Villar factory in Havana—a shape (front-mark) named "Excepcionales de Rothschilds."

In part, Duke's interest in cigars—like his interest in plug—was defensive. Around the turn of the century, when paper cigarettes were not only overtaxed and undersold but threatened with restrictive legislation, he began production of *Recruit*, a cigarette-sized cigar, as a hedge.

For cigars as for cigarettes, the great growth impetus seems to have been furnished by wars. When Wash Duke was peddling *Pro Bono Publico* in his Conestoga wagon, the per capita consumption of large cigars* was around twenty-five. In five years it went to forty-three; when the old American Tobacco Company was formed in 1890, it was almost sixty-five; and in 1901, the founding year for American Cigar, it was seventy-four. Perhaps the Spanish-American war gave the luxury roll an extra push; from a national sales total of 4,063,200,000 in 1897, the business went to 6,786,400,000 in 1903—an increase of just 67% in six years.

Slow roll

Although cigar sales held at seven or eight billion a year until 1920, the brown roll was being left behind by the white one. Its use did not keep up with population growth, and 1907's per capita consumption of eighty-six was to be the peak (current per capita consumption is less than forty). And after

*Those weighing more than three pounds per thousand.

Before 1901, the year James Duke founded American Cigar, most brown rolls were turned out by small operators or retailers. At the century's turn there were about 20,000 of them. Employees worked at home or in tiny back rooms of shops like the one above.

Samuel Gompers began as a cigar maker. He argued for better conditions in cigar factories, went on to found the American Federation of Labor itself.

Handmade Spanish cigars (above) were the standard of excellence after the Revolution. As late as 1930 the best were made in Cuba in the Spanish fashion.

Marshall made his famous remark about the "really good five cent cigar" during Wilson's first term. Today, a good ten cent cigar is a prime achievement.

Many cigar machines were tried and failed. This device, advertised for sale in 1857 by John Prentice of New York, used "pedals moved by the feet" for its power.

1907, even Duke must have had doubts about his new cigar empire. The next two years saw losses of 8.5% and 7.7% on his Havana business. And in 1910, on sales of a billion cigars (of the nation's seven billion), the profit on Havana product was a mere 5.1%, on domestic cigars 5.8%. In those years, before the corporate income tax was levied, such margins were positively whiskerlike.

The reason for these relatively low profits was twofold. First, the hand-labor nature of cigar-making permitted family enterprises to invent and sell small brands at prices which reflected less labor cost than the least skilled workers could command in the open market. And second, quality of product was difficult to detect except over a period of time. The small fly-by-night roller who ran out of good leaf usually had no compunction about degrading his brand name—or if he had, it was easy for him to change it. Since only a small percentage of smokers were *connoisseurs* in any degree, the maintenance of consistent leaf standards was not a guarantee of quick financial success.

In any event, it is unlikely Duke or his associates shed too many tears when the Supreme Court halved his cigar business. From the quality point of view, dissolution left The American Tobacco Company with the fine old Cuban names; it was mainly the domestic brands that were awarded to the reconstituted Lorillard company.

During the tenure of Percival Hill, the cigar department was probably his most static. There were the domestic brands remaining after dissolution—mainly *Cremo*, *Chancellor* and *Roi-Tan*. And there were the clear Havana types, *La Corona*, *Antonio y Cleopatra*, *Cabañas*, *La Vencedora*, *Villar y Villar*—all made in Cuba. As the import duty on these climbed, the market narrowed. And while the great number of cigar makers dwindled—to 17,000 in 1917, 14,600 in 1921, and 10,800 in 1925—so did per capita consumption.

Patterson's machine

It was during the early twenties that a glimmer of hope for five cent cigars first developed. A long line of Rube Goldberg contraptions had failed to do for cigars what the Bonsack machine had done for cigarettes. There were, to be sure, several devices which supplemented manual dexterity if they did not replace it entirely—bunchers, molds, stemmers, suction tables to hold the wrapper for the roller's knife. Toward the end of War I, however, an "alumnus" of J. B. Duke's trust came up with a workable mechanism. Rufus L. Patterson, president of the American Machine & Foundry Company, had produced improved cigarette machines, some of which are still in use. His 1917 cigar maker laid the filler, applied binder and wrapper and even turned the ends, yielding 480 complete cigars in an hour. This seemed to open the way for a realization of Marshall's half-serious desire, and machine-made cigars zoomed. By 1926, the first year of George Washington Hill's presidency, one cigar in every five was mechanically rolled. Four years later, the proportion was one in three.

The case for Cremo

Impelled by the same vision of volume which brought J. B. Duke to New York, G. W. Hill put the weight of his advertising behind one of the old brands, *Cremo*, made on the new Patterson machines to sell for a nickel. It was, in fact, promoted as the "5c cigar that America needed." In his enthusiasm for the advantages of the new crush-proof, foil-wrapped cigar made with scientific purity, Hill talked plainly—a little too plainly, according to his critics. "Spit," went the classic *Cremo* ad, "is a horrid word. But it is worse on the end of your cigar . . . Why run the risk of cigars made by dirty, yellowed fingers and tipped in spit? Remember, more than half of all cigars made in this country are still made *by hand*, and therefore subject to the risk of spit!"

Hill's personal popularity was not helped by this ultra-vivid copy. But regardless of his choice of words, the message was both logical and true. After two years, *Cremo* sales reached a peak annual rate of 1,400,000,000—fully 23% of the entire cigar market. At that level it could have justified the heavy advertising expense behind it. But the cigar competition, thoroughly alarmed, took drastic measures. One popular brand, visibly larger than *Cremo*, reduced its price from three-for-20c to a nickel, with marked effects on *Cremo*'s volume. At this juncture, too, a distinct downward trend appeared in the nation's consumption not only of cigars, but of cigarettes and chewing tobacco as well (*see chart, page 93*). Even in 1929 cigarettes accounted for over 80% of the Com-

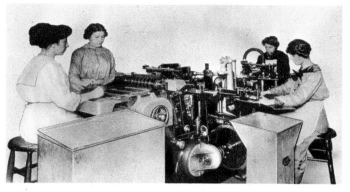

After the 1918 Armistice, American Machine & Foundry machine got a factory trial. Invented by Rufus L. Patterson, it now makes virtually all U. S. cigars.

Albert Gold came to American Cigar's Trenton plant in 1903, trained a cadre of cigarmakers. In 1932 he moved La Corona production from Cuba to New Jersey.

To do this, Company built a new plant duplicating the humidity of Cuba. Alfred E. Smith, presidential candidate in 1928, helped G. W. Hill dedicate plant.

pany's revenue, and George Hill abandoned the dream of *Cremo* volume. To get rid of his huge inventory he cut the price to three for a dime. At the same time *Cremo*'s advertising budget was sharply curtailed and this, together with the abrupt downpricing, constituted a strategic retreat from the nickel battlefield.

From mass to class

The *Cremo* campaign was by no means the whole show so far as American Tobacco's cigar business was concerned. Although that attempt to edge downward into the mass market was written off,

Chancellor and *Roi-Tan* remained as American's entries among the domestic grades. And the fine cigar field was still an American domain. Most prominent in the clear Havana department were the famous *La Corona* line and *Antonio y Cleopatra*, mildest of the clear Havanas. Along with *Bock, Cabañas* and *Villar y Villar, La Corona* was being made in Cuba as it had been for almost a century. It was, and still is, the world's standard of excellence, the ultimate luxury product in a *de luxe* field.

The market itself was split into literally hundreds of segments. At one point *La Corona* alone was made in no less than 1,300 different sizes, of which

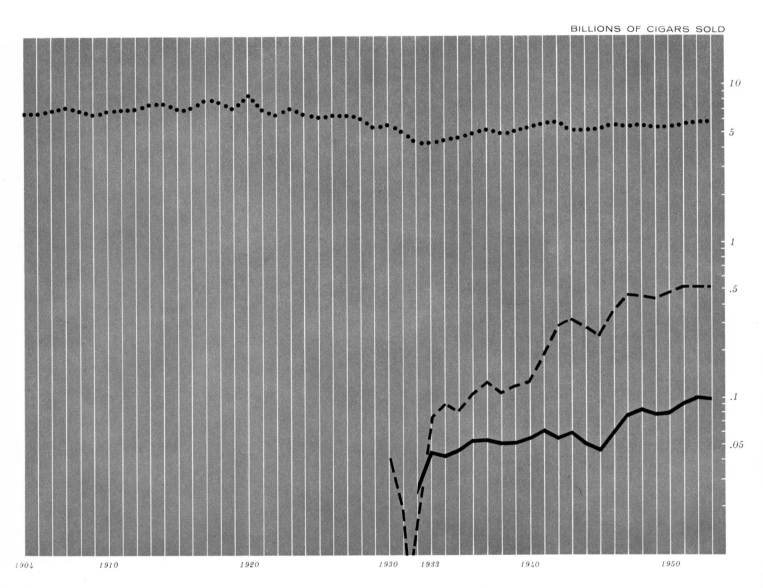

BILLIONS OF CIGARS SOLD

10
5
1
.5
.1
.05

1904   1910   1920   1930 1933   1940   1950

Fewer cigars are sold today than in 1904. But the Company's clear Havana brands have quadrupled since 1932. Plotted on a logarithmic scale to show rates of change, the dotted line shows sales of all cigars,

the solid line combined sales of La Corona, Antonio y Cleopatra, Henry Clay, Bock, Vencedora and Villar. El Roi-Tan, Company's top domestic cigar, has shown even faster growth (broken line) and is now the leading 10c cigar.

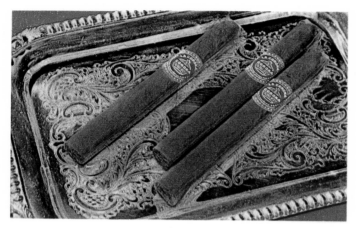

Best known of American's clear Havana brands is La Corona. Its most famous shape is the Corona, making "La Corona Corona" a synonym for the finest in cigars.

What Champagne country is to wine Cuba is to cigars. West of Havana the island crooks downward; this end, —the Vuelta Abajo or "down turn"—grows top leaf.

some 260 were standard production shapes and the remainder custom-rolled for individual smokers in uneconomic batches of a few hundred at a time. No wonder Hill, bothered by the demise of *Cremo*, dismissed the cigar trade as unrewarding and resumed his concentration on *Lucky Strike*.

A further factor squeezed the famous old brands into the limited upper reaches of the market— duty on finished cigars, which was exactly 900% higher than duty on baled leaf. Albert Gregg, who took over in 1932 as President of American Cigar, estimated that the *La Corona* Perfecto, then selling at three for a dollar, could be reduced to half that price if manufactured in the United States from the same tobacco. Similarly, the line leader, *La Corona* Corona, could be sold at three for a dollar if rolled domestically as against a 60c price tag for the imported product. So it was logical that in 1932 L. S. Houston, Pat H. Gorman, Sr., and Albert Gold (later named chief of cigar manufacture) were authorized by Hill and Gregg to build a rolling plant in Trenton. They air-conditioned it to duplicate the atmosphere of Havana, where humidity averages 80%. Although the press expressed some doubts at the time, the shift in manufacturing site was no gamble: production of *Antonio y Cleopatra* had been moved successfully from Tampa to Trenton two years before. Brought closer within reach of the average American cigar smoker, *La Corona* began a growth climb that is still continuing. Along with the Company's other brands of clear Havana leaf—the first nationally distributed cigars manufactured in

Within Vuelta province of Pinar del Rio, best leaf comes from District One. American's subsidiary owns and cultivates more land there than all its rivals.

District One dominance springs from rich soil, 80% humidity, bright sun—and the local tradition that "everyone is a good father, especially to tobacco!"

Seedlings planted in October are weeded and watered every day. After two months they are six inches high and ready for transplanting from seedbed to field.

Wrapper leaf is grown under cheesecloth. This makes plants taller and leaves larger and lighter. Most cigar smokers prefer a smooth, light green wrapper.

Removal of flower buds is called "topping," channels full nourishment into leaves. Each shadegrown plant reaches six-foot height, yields about sixteen leaves.

bond—it now accounts for almost a fourth of the fine cigar market.*

One and only district

Like the rise of the paper cigarette, based on the development of Bright tobacco in North Carolina and White Burley in Kentucky, the growing market for clear Havana cigars has its roots in good earth. The choicest plantation land in Pinar del Rio surrounds the little villages of San Juan y Martinez and San Luis, known as District One. Most of this district's leaf land is owned or leased by the American Tobacco subsidiary furnishing leaf for *La Corona*.

The crop is harvested in February and March, after which the loamy brown soil is permitted to rest. Heaps of fertilizer are left on the ground to decompose, and in June it is spread over the fields and harrowed. Heavy summer rains work the nourishment into the earth; then the top soil is loosened again and refertilized with cottonseed meal and potash. The entire process of revitalization is supervised by a scientific laboratory near San Juan y Martinez.

Before the crop is laid out, the fields are given a fall cleaning. Two or three plowings and harrowings break up the soil to a powdery softness, and any dried weeds are pulled out. Sometime in October the tobacco seedlings are planted in special beds which are irrigated every night and weeded by hand every day. By December the best of these seedlings—about six inches high—are ready for transplanting to the fields proper.

Some tobacco, destined for use as wrapper, is grown under great sheets of cheesecloth stretched above the ground like so many flat circus tents. Partial screening from the sun makes the leaves lighter, larger and finer in texture; although their flavor does not differ from that of sun-grown leaf, light-colored cigars are more pleasing to the smoker's eye. Each year an amount of Cuban acreage equal to more than a thousand football fields is covered with cloth to produce shade-grown wrappers for *La Corona*.

Whether grown in sun or shade, the tiny

---

*The "fine cigar market" is defined by the tax classifications F and G, comprising cigars selling for more than 15c at retail. The other classes include A, cigars selling for 2.5c or less; B, 2.6 to 4c; C, 4.1 to 6c; D, 6.1 to 8c; and E, 8.1 to 15c.

plants are inspected every day. The sucker leaves are removed as are the flower buds, for all the plant's strength must be funneled into the leaves. There will be ten or twelve large leaves on each sun-grown plant, fourteen or sixteen on the shade-grown. In the two months it takes these plants to reach four and six feet, respectively, the soil is constantly being hoed, irrigated, sprayed and fertilized. Finally, in February and March, the leaves themselves are gathered.

"The *La Corona* worker," goes a saying, "is a good father—especially to his tobacco." Wrapper leaves are pampered like children, removed individually as they mature and taken first to the drying barn. There, strung in pairs on cotton thread, they are hung on poles to cure. This curing is mostly "controlled" by fire, which renders the wrappers extra light ("golden claro"). Sun-grown leaves are removed in pairs with part of the plant stalk still holding them together. They are hung out in the sun for a time before they are put into the drying barn to be air-cured or "natural-cured."

All this, however, is only a beginning. When the rains begin in May, the dried leaves again become moist and pliable enough to be handled. For a month they are piled in the farm warehouse to "heat" in rectangular stacks. This induces fermentation, and the temperature is kept under 120 degrees to prevent damage to the leaf. This stage is called "bulking" or "sweating," words which are used in cigarette manufacture with a somewhat different meaning.

"in their time"

Always soft and pliable, so that they may be handled without damage, the leaves are then sorted by size, kind of leaf, and the probable curing time. The graders separate the dry, extra dry, thin, pliable, medium, medium heavy and heavy leaves, each of which requires a different period of curing in bale—anywhere from six months to three years. "Our tobaccos," say the plantation managers, "are worked in their time."

The graded leaves are first tied in bunches or "hands"; these are kept for a while in large cedar boxes and then tied in bundles of four called "carots." Eighty of these carots make a bale, which is wrapped in stiff Royal Palm leaves and tied with fiber of majagua bark. Each bale is exactly the same as the

Ripe leaves are removed one by one in February and March. Wrapper is "control-cured" with artificial heat to achieve desirable "golden claro" lightness.

Sun-grown leaf, used as filler and binder, is hung in the sun for a time, then moved to an air-curing barn. In two or three months, it turns rich brown.

All tobacco in La Corona and Antonio y Cleopatra comes from Cuba. American's were the first cigars manufactured in bond having national distribution.

Graders separate leaves by size and type. Cure time varies with grade up to three years. Forty to sixty leaves tie into a "hand," four hands into a "carot."

After a cedar box siesta at the packing barn, leaf is moistened to make it pliable. This conditioning or "casing" is repeated often during manufacture.

Bale of cigar leaf holds eighty carots, wrapped in "yaguas" or leaf-ends of Royal Palm. One bale of fine wrapper may sell for over a thousand dollars.

next, down to the last fiber knot, and weighs between sixty-five and one hundred pounds.

During their long siesta in the warehouses of Havana, the bales are turned from time to time to take the weight off the bottom leaves. Toward the end of the curing time, a carot or two is pulled out of a bale; it is smelled, felt, and even smoked to determine whether it is ready for use. If so, the stems are removed—by hand—and the pure tobacco then gets its final six-month "barbacoa cure" in barrels. ("Barbacoa" derives from the old Indian word for a low-ceilinged room.) This final step, however, is omitted in the case of wrapper leaf, which is too delicate to be given the additional handling. It will be stemmed at the factory.

Once more wrapped in "yaguas," as the stiff lower extremities of palm leaves are called, the leaves are burlapped and shipped to the United States.

Left handed and right

Again "cased" or conditioned with moisture, the filler and wrapper leaves are laid out for rolling into a wide variety of shapes and lengths. Each bundle of long filler is rolled in one-half of a wrapper leaf; and because the smooth, silky top side must always be on the outside, the rollers and the cigars they make are either "left handed" or "right handed." After passing inspection, *La Coronas* are seasoned another two months in rooms lined with Cuban cedar. Wrapped in cellophane and banded, they are then boxed. Even the cases in which the boxes go out to the wholesaler are lined with protective material which varies with the climate to which *La Coronas* are being sent. American Tobacco salesmen follow them all the way to the retail counter, seeing that they are not exposed to excessive heat or dryness, cautioning the tobacconist against displaying them alongside candy lest the redolent Havana leaf absorb alien odors.

This kind of follow-up is, of course, vital to attaining distribution. Recent surveys show that more American Tobacco *de luxe* cigars are displayed in the nation's showcases than all others combined. This point-of-sale penetration has been carried one step further than the tobacconist: during the four years ended in 1953, no fewer than 70,000 cigar smokers were "sampled" by A. Gordon Findlay's field men. Each received a miniature cigar box containing five *La Coronas* or *Antonio y Cleopatras* after a personal chat about the details of production that make them "supreme the world over."

Volume vantage

These details are just as responsible for the growth curve as field promotion. They make possible volume acceptance, but they in turn are made possible by volume production. In the simple but crucial matter of combining tobaccos prior to rolling, the Havana leaf is divided into five kinds. Each factory worker must take a certain proportion of each kind to "bunch" every batch of fifty. The normal course of manufacture, even in Cuba itself, is to spread out all the tobacco in a single pile, and the normal result is that workers pick the easiest-rolling leaf first. And it is volume on the plantation which makes selective aging possible and makes "Our tobaccos are worked in their time" more than a slogan. It is a curious fact that only mass production permits control of a kind impossible for hand craftsmen. Since 1952, for instance, an extra step has been added to leaf preparation. After newly-arrived wrapper is unbaled and moistened, the leaves are hung with the tips down so that any extra water will drain off. This avoids dark streaks—water stains—in the finished cigars.

But maintaining uniform and high quality depends more upon people than upon plans and procedures. Keeping the Company's people particular is the prime task of the Company's management. To impress on his rollers the importance of blend, the head of one *Antonio y Cleopatra* plant recently had a batch of cigars made using only one kind of leaf. Smoking these unblended samples drove home the point better than words could have done. Since many of the plant's people are women, some special corn bread was baked, without salt. A few mouthfuls illustrated the same point on the distaff side.

Sometimes customers must be kept particular too, for fine cigars will not take care of themselves. Last December President Paul Hahn dined at a well-known New York restaurant, one of those "where particular people congregate." The after-dinner Havanas were brought to the tables on open trays, and one tray was left on a stand where a waiter

Baled leaf is frequently inspected by warehousemen who may make a sample cigar to test readiness for rolling. La Corona tobaccos are worked "in their time."

Final cure for filler and binder leaf is in barrel. Each is slotted for ventilation, and a center well permits warehousemen to check inside temperatures.

The "barbacoa cure"—so-called from the Indian name for a low-ceilinged room—completes process of leaf fermentation. It lasts six months or more.

Cured, aged, graded and re-baled, the leaf leaves for the U. S. One bale contains enough filler for 7,000 clear Havanas or enough wrapper for 22,000.

Inside as well as out, the Trenton rolling plant is a bit of transplanted Havana. Many of the men who superintend the casing and sorting are Cuban born.

Blending is carefully controlled. Incoming leaf is regraded, for even within a line every shape has its own blend of heavy, medium and lighter leaves.

worked his flaming magic on a stack of *crepes suzette.* Hahn suffered through this performance only once: shortly thereafter, particular smokers noted that the restaurateur's cigars were housed in a cedar tray hooded with transparent lucite.

New shape for cigars

Like the cigarette brands, cigars have tended to narrow to a relatively small number in contrast to the former long lists. During Percival Hill's early years as President, the American Cigar subsidiary marketed some twenty-one 5c cigars including *Cremo, Anna Held, Figaro, Little Chancellor, Henner, Cubanola, Geo. Peabody, Hoffman House* and others. In addition to *Chancellor,* the high grade domestic line included *El Gutan, Ben Mirza, Caswell Club* and *La Gerania.* The blended Havanas included *Tiberius* and *Osmundo* as well as *El Roi-Tan.* The "International Brands" included *La Meridiana, La Carolina* and *Manual Garcia* as well as the *Cabañas, La Corona, Henry Clay, Villar y Villar* and *Bock* lines. During those years all the Internationals were made in Havana; seven other brands were made of all-Havana leaf in this country—*Antonio y Cleopatra, Flor de Cuba, La Esperanza, El Principe de Gales* and *Fama Universal* in Tampa, *El Belmont* and *La Belle Imperia* in New Orleans. In all, there were thirty-seven different cigar names, as against ten today.

But to make these ten cigar brands is vastly more complicated than the manufacture of fifteen cigarette brands, the current number. *La Corona* comes in twenty-four shapes, *El Roi-Tan* in five, *Antonio y Cleopatra* in nine. Since dimensions greatly affect smoking characteristics, each shape has its own blend, its own proportions of the various leaf types. And unlike cigarettes, which have produced only two major sizes in fifty years, new cigar shapes appear and old ones disappear almost yearly.

Although *La Corona, Cabañas, Bock* and *Antonio y Cleopatra* still dominate the clear Havana market, the machine age has reshaped the cigar business as a whole—just as George Hill anticipated. Almost 90% of the cigars consumed in this country are relatively inexpensive imitations of the Vuelta Abajo brown roll. By the same token, three-fourths of American Tobacco's cigar sales are in the popular-priced *Roi-Tan* series. (This year, the line is being rounded out with the revival of green-boxed *Chancellors*, to compete with the more expensive domestic cigars in classes E and F. One of the Company's oldest cigar names, *Chancellor* was taken out of production during the stringent years of War II.)

The growth of *Roi-Tan* is one of the unsung phenomena of the modern tobacco industry. In the pit depression year of 1932 hardly more than 6,000,-000 were sold on the domestic market. By 1953, unit sales had increased 8,400% to over half a billion, and *Roi-Tan* sales alone accounted for 9% of all cigars withdrawn from U. S. factories. Most *Roi-Tans* are priced at 10c and the cigar, led by its Perfecto Extra shape, is the leading seller at that price. Made of Havana and Pennsylvania filler, *Roi-Tan* has a Wisconsin binder and a Connecticut shadegrown wrapper, much of the latter grown by the Company's own subsidiary, Hatheway-Steane. It is manufactured in Wilkes-Barre, Scranton, Charleston, Ashley, Louisville and Philadelphia.

One of *Roi-Tan*'s distinguished characteristics is the punctured head: it is advertised as "the cigar that breathes." Although pre-puncturing has spread to rival domestic brands and even to the Company's *Antonio y Cleopatra* Havana line, it was a *La Corona* cigar—the slender Eloisas Listas—in which the hole first appeared, sometime during the nineteenth century. Jobbers have often inquired why the *La Corona* line is not punched too. The answer to this question, as to many others about product design and packaging, goes back to the ultimate consumer. Whether he is called *connoisseur* or simply creature of habit, the smoker is apt to regard his pipe or cigar more as a companion than an expendable bit of agricultural produce. He resents change, and may regard even an improvement as "evidence" of downgrading in quality.

Clearly claro

George W. Hill, whose career spanned the metamorphosis of American Tobacco from the plug and smoking era to the age of the cigarette, grew to respect this nostalgic attachment.* Hill once received a complaint from a smoker in Florence, Kentucky,

---

*He was notoriously reluctant to make changes in package design, and refused to kill even the most superannuated minor brands.

Each whole shadegrown leaf makes two wrappers, one half spiraled clockwise around its cigar, the other half counterclockwise. The smooth side is outside.

Most La Coronas are made and wrapped by machine, which does a better job than hand-rollers. Hand labor, however, is vital for curing, casing and sorting.

Shapes too long to fit machines are made by hand. These are the very large, extra long types such as Aristocrats, After Dinners, Premiers and Campanas.

Before cellophaning, La Coronas are seasoned in cedar finishing room. Here they "intermarry," and achieve uniform aroma. Albert Gold, above, retired in 1953.

Cigars are packed for uniform color. It takes four days to color-select, band, wrap, pack and label each box; it is four years from seedbed to smoker.

to the effect that *Roi-Tan* quality was deteriorating. "We have a Roi-Tan Club here in Florence," the letter read, "and our members have tried every one of the shapes in which *Roi-Tan* is made." Anyone who knew the precise number of shapes in the line, reasoned Hill, was no crank. Down to Kentucky went one of the cigar executives to investigate. The trouble? Dark cigars. A shipment of "colorado" cigars with reddish brown wrappers had gone to Florence in place of the usual "claros"—the same cigar but with a wrapper of light, greenish-brown leaf. So sensitive to color are cigar smokers that most demand the lightest possible wrapper, feeling that the darker outside leaves denote a heavier smoking quality. Vet-

erans of the brown roll, though, testify that the darker wrappers—even the nearly black "maduro"—taste better than the light ones. For them, *La Coronas* are supplied in red-tabbed boxes signifying sun-cured wrappers.

But although fine cigars are the quality leader of American's product list (President Paul Hahn, like his predecessor Vincent Riggio, is an inveterate smoker of *Antonio y Cleopatra*), the more portable, more convenient cigarette is the everyday choice of the public, accounting at present for 95% of American Tobacco's dollar sales. And even before it attained its place in the lips and hearts of Americans, it was the choice of George Washington Hill.

Cigars have their own separate sales force, headed by A. Gordon Findlay. Manufacturing supervision of all cigar lines came under a single head early in 1954.

Cigar merchandising extends all the way to retail showcase. If they are too dry, too hot, too moist, or mixed with other items, aroma will be impaired.

NATURE IN THE RAW

GEORGE WASHINGTON HILL was one of the very few men who become legends even while they are still alive. Like Paul Bunyan, John Henry, and many another legendary figure, Hill was a "natcheral man." This, perhaps, is the best explanation of his raw genius, his frequent disregard of protocol, his driving impatience. Unlike his father, Percival Hill, George was not a mild man. But nature in the raw, as Hill himself put it, is seldom mild.

Despite his early training in leaf-buying and manufacturing, Hill was too impatient a man ever to really master those skills—although he could appreciate them in others. And despite his tutelage under James Duke and Percival Hill, G. W. differed from them in another aspect of management—delegating authority. Here also his innate impatience impelled him to make all the decisions himself.

In an organization less fortified with seasoned tobacco men, Hill's particular talents might not have flourished as they did. But he was surrounded by a core of proud, professional experts, many of them veterans of Duke's combination. They did not always admire Hill's bravura manner, but they had to admire his salesmanship. And Hill's instinctive empathy for the Common Man plus his flair for showmanship were just what was needed during the flowering of

brand land, with its critical dependence on advertising. He could sell cigarettes.

Young Hill did not take full command immediately after his father's death. A new position, board Chairman, was created in December, 1925, and for 40 months it was filled by Junius Parker. "The Judge," as Parker was called, enjoyed a reputation as the dean of the industry. As an aide to Duke since 1905 and Company Counsel since 1912, Parker knew the business from the inside out. Although the by-laws did not designate him "chief executive officer" in 1925, he acted as a steadying influence on George Hill—not only as Chairman but even after his official retirement in 1929.

Although some of his stockholders were to hale Hill into court to defend his high salary, he was true to them in his own fashion. Hill did not make a practice of attending annual stockholders' meetings, on the ground that chattering with the minority who attended was a waste of his time, and therefore not in the best interests of the majority who paid him to run the Company. He felt more qualified to make any decision than anybody else partly because he spent more time than anybody else on the business. In his Irvington home there was a radio in every room, where he could tune in his own commercials or those

Lucky Strike trademark, first registered in arm-and-hammer design, was changed by R. A. Patterson

of Richmond to red bullseye. Duke invested in the Patterson company in 1903, bought it out in 1905.

of rivals. In the garden there were tobacco plants.

One of the first things he did on acceding to the presidency of American Tobacco was to clear the decks for concentrated action. Within a year of his appointment he leased several minor cigarette brands, including *Herbert Tareyton*, to George Whelan's Union Tobacco Company. American still made the brands, but Whelan worried about selling them.

When Hill took over, the big brand—*Lucky Strike*—needed his attention. Once-potent names—*Sovereign, Sweet Caporal, Lord Salisbury*—were losing

their earlier vigor. *Lucky* was the third entry in the Big Three race, and both *Camel* and *Chesterfield* had made good use of their head start, though Liggett & Myers appeared to be giving its maximum push to Turkish blends even after War I. *Camel*, of course, did not labor under this handicap, since it was Reynolds' only cigarette. Possibly for this reason it accounted for 41% of the national output in 1925, *vs.* *Chesterfield*'s 24% and 16% for *Lucky Strike*.

Late in that year Hill retained Albert D. Lasker, whose agency, Lord & Thomas, brought fame

Before 1940 Lucky Strike label had the large bullseye on front, a smaller version on back.

and national distribution to Sunkist oranges, Kleenex, Pepsodent, Quaker Oats and Frigidaire among others. Like Hill, Lasker relied on inspired word-jockeying to stamp his message on the public mind; and like Hill, Lasker had no patience with bland "reminder advertising" that lacked the "reason why" element. The two made an effective team.

Real live women

Their first break with tradition was the use of women in testimonial advertisements, real live American women like actress Alice Brady. Other tobacco companies had daintily skirted the question of lady smokers by using foreign-born opera singers, veiled Orientals, and imaginary lady pirates in ragged shorts. Since millions of American women were already confirmed smokers, Hill and Lasker discarded the roundabout approaches and made their appeal direct. This done, they searched their minds for new variations and settled, typically, on one of Hill's ideas —"Reach for a *Lucky* Instead of a Sweet."

"I was riding out to my home," Hill later recalled, "and I got to 110th Street and Fifth Avenue; I was sitting in the car and I looked at the corner, and there was a great big stout lady chewing gum. And there was a taxicab—it was in the summertime— coming the other way. I thought I was human and I looked, and there was a young lady sitting in the taxicab with a long cigarette holder in her mouth, and she had a very good figure. I didn't know what she was smoking . . .

"But right then and there it hit me; there was the lady that was stout and chewing, and there was the young girl that was slim and smoking a cigarette. 'Reach for a *Lucky* Instead of a Sweet.' There it was, right in front of you."

The campaign broke in 1928 and in two years there was *Lucky Strike*, right in front of *Camel* and *Chesterfield*, with sales of 42,000,000,000 cigarettes for 1930. The candy industry was more than slightly outraged, although the theme had been used before (in 1891, Lydia Pinkham urged ladies to "Reach for a vegetable instead of a sweet").

Lucky Strike continued to lead the packs; in 1931 its sales of 44,500,000,000 were some 11,200,-000,000 units ahead of the No. 2 brand. The climb was doubtless made possible by effective advertising, but it depended on more than Hill's choice of words. The taste was, and is, unique—the toasted *Lucky* has always been easy to identify in a blindfold test.

But toward the end of the year, two widely-held notions were exploded: one, that the precipitous Wall Street crash of 1929 didn't necessarily presage a drastic business depression; and two, that the cigarette business was "depression-proof." As wages, prices, jobs and purchasing power declined, so did

1940 label duplicated front and back, added white bullseye ring, cleaned lettering.

War II made chromium for green ink scarce. Experimental "extended green" was not used.

cigarette consumption. Among the lowered prices was the price of leaf tobacco, and this led among other things to the "ten centers" or "economy brands."

In two years, the average price of flue-cured cigarette leaf had tumbled from 19c to 12c per pound, and Burley had fallen from 25c to 11c. Since leaf is the major cost item in cigarette making, it was now possible to market a smokable 10c cigarette. Thus the pit year of depression, 1932, saw a not-very-gradual rise in the sales of cheap cigarettes; by the end of the

year, one out of every five packs sold was a ten center. At the same time, consumption of all cigarettes dropped a cool 10,000,000,000, a market shrinkage of 9%.

Statistics on manufactured cigarettes, however, do not tell the whole story. For in the same pit year enough cigarettes were home-rolled (based on the increased use of cigarette paper) to boost cigarette *smoking* by an estimated 10,000,000,000 units. In the thick of this was old *Bull Durham*, whose sales

Actual war revision in 1942 eliminated green. Gold ink around bullseye became grey.

"Reach for a Lucky" theme in 1928 was among Hill's most effective, pushed Lucky Strike to top by 1930.

Same theme in sophisticated format was going strong in 1933, with "good taste" replacing "it's toasted."

increased from 6,000,000 pounds in 1930 to over 15,000,000 pounds in 1932. The increase in *Bull Durham* alone was enough to make 3,500,000,000 cigarettes, cancelling out almost a fourth of the dip in tailor-mades. And the muslin bags with the bull-headed tags were still going strong in 1940, when nearly 20,000,000 pounds were sold—enough to make 7,000,000,000 roll-your-owns. At a nickel, a sack of the Bull was equivalent to 33 cigarettes in the hands of a skilled roller. Breadlines or no breadlines, the nation was not willing to give up cigarettes.

Luxury or staple?

While the nation was in the throes of the "shorts," purchases of staples and luxuries alike shrunk alarmingly. But it is interesting to note that tobacco consumption, which peaked at 7.18 pounds per capita in 1929, slipped off very gradually to 6.01

pounds in 1932 and in four more years was up to 7.16 pounds again. Comparing this relatively mild slump to that experienced in other lines, one might well conclude that tobacco is more necessity than luxury—a conclusion that the nation's generals reiterate at the outbreak of every war. Perhaps the best expression of tobacco's place in war, in peace, and in depression—though not, perhaps, the most literary—was the immortal line of 1914: "While you've a lucifer to light your fag, smile, boys, that's the style!"

The depression, which dramatically demonstrated the solace to be derived from tobacco, also witnessed a decline of the anti-tobacco crusades that seem to accompany times of boom. In 1937 North Dakota wiped from its statute books an old law forbidding smoking in public conveyances or restaurants. And in spite of one zealot's claim that smokers tended to beget more daughters than sons (the overall birth

Blue Boar, an old Marburg Branch mixture, was given a ham flavoring as late as the 1920s. But even after the ham was omitted, the Boar blend continued to win pipe smokers, became American's top "high grade" mix.

This was the first "Half and Half" trademark, used in 1873 for a pipe tobacco sold by Francis S. Kinney.

Translated from numbers into words, the brand name was affixed in 1926 to a new pipe mixture—half Buckingham, half Lucky Strike smoking tobacco. With the aid of advertising and the depression surge of manufactured tobacco, the blend became number four

proportions are the other way around), the sound and the fury of the twenties subsided. Even while the counterblasters fulminated over the steep rise in tobacco consumption, the vital statistics were revealing greater longevity for Americans of every class. In the end, the pronouncements of doom signified nothing.

Pipe lines

While *Lucky Strike* was being built up during the younger Hill's first years as President, non-cigarette lines were not ignored. *Half and Half*, currently the Company's leading smoking tobacco brand, was revived in 1926 and in five years achieved a fifth of *Bull Durham*'s poundage. The name itself was not new: in 1873 Francis S. Kinney had brought out a smoking tobacco with the numerical mark, "½ & ½." Following the competitive mode of the day, the little Hernsheim company registered *'Alf and 'Alf* as a trade name in 1880. During the early 1900s American Tobacco's Marburg Branch made a *Half and Half* of "Fine Perique and Virginia Mixed," among a number of other tobacco brands including *Little Brown Jug, Little Flirt, Little Red Riding Hood, Little Flora* and *Little Dorrit*. As its name suggests, the modern *Half and Half* mixture incorporated both Burley and Bright—the former represented by *Lucky Strike* smoking tobacco, the latter by the old *Buckingham* blend. By 1939 the new blend was selling almost 8,000,000 pounds a year. This was about 40% of *Bull Durham*'s product weight and gave *Half and*

among the top five's smoking brands by 1939. Half and Half sales then amounted to 40% of Bull Durham's. Modern Half and Half label still bears traces of the Lucky Strike design, though Lucky Strike pipe tobacco is a separate blend and is still sold by the Company.

Depression revived demand for roll-your-own smokes, upped Bull Durham sales to the equivalent of seven
billion cigarettes. The Bull was advertised only by 24-sheet posters, of which this was most widely used.

Half the fourth position among the top five's smoking tobacco brands. It must be added, though, that the Bull sold nearly 20,000,000 pounds in that year without any advertising whatever, while *Half and Half* had an ad budget amounting to 3c a pound.

Another pipe tobacco which made the transition from a specialty to a "universal blend" was *Blue Boar*. As late as 1923 that mixture, an old Marburg brand, was being given a ham flavor by exposing it to the aroma of smoking hams. Like the chocolate in *Tuxedo*, the ham hocks used to make *Blue Boar* have disappeared. But the mixture itself, a rich, rough-cut and rather strong blend of Perique, Lata-

kia, Burley and Bright leaf, has outlasted many others and is now the Company's top premium pipe tobacco.

Blue Boar, however, is very much the exception. Even in the days of Richmond's glory as the No. 1 tobacco manufacturing center, individual high-grade pipe mixtures had never run to any volume. Said a Company booklet during the twenties: "The greatest experimenter in the world is the user of smoking tobacco. No matter how strongly wedded a man may be to one particular mixture, back in the deepest recesses of his mind there is always the fear that he is overlooking a good bet. . . . ." So

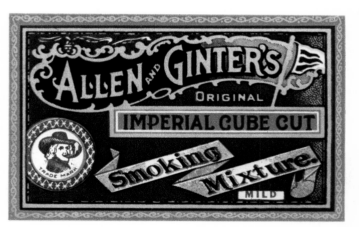

Individual pipe tobacco blends, however, rarely gained big volume. Imperial Cube Cut and the Arcadia mixture were among 27 high-grade brands made by the Company in 1931; the number was 25 as late as 1940, is 17 today. American Tobacco made 99 popular-priced smoking and
chewing brands in 1931, still makes 45 of them. Pipe fanciers are generally reluctant to change from their accustomed blends, which accounts for the long list. Also, pipe mixtures are made in a wider variety of blends than cigarettes, use many more leaf types.

specialists in the field, like the old Falk Company, had to turn out a long list of brands in order to achieve respectable total volume. "It's a small brand, but there are those who love it" best describes the typical pipe puffer's attachment to the mixture of his choice. In 1931, for example, American Tobacco marketed 126 smoking tobaccos, 27 of them in the high-grade category. Even today, the price list includes no fewer than 17 high-grade mixtures and 45 "smoking and chewing" brands, most of which are suitable for use in a pipe. Among the latter, *Compass, Cutty Pipe, Five Brothers, Peerless (Adams), Standard (Adams), Tuxedo, Liberty, Ivanhoe* and *Virgin Leaf (McAlpin's)* are strong favorites. Among the high-grades are the old *Arcadia* mixture, celebrated in James Barrie's "My Lady Nicotine," *Imperial Cube Cut,* still made in both mild and medium strengths, *Personal, Pinkussohn's Potpourri, Old English Curve Cut,* and *Serene.* In 1930, 1931 and 1932, as sales of

The old Kinney factory in Richmond was renovated in 1930 and put to use as a stemmery and redrying plant. Same year saw completion of a new factory across the street. It now produces 25% of Company's cigarettes.

tailor-made cigarettes dropped off, sales of smoking tobacco climbed. Since "package terbaker" is a not

No raw tobaccos in Luckies —that's why they're so mild

WE buy the finest, the very finest tobaccos in all the world—but that does not explain why folks everywhere regard Lucky Strike as the mildest cigarette. The fact is, we never overlook the truth that "Nature in the Raw is Seldom Mild"—so these fine tobaccos, after proper aging and mellowing, are then given the benefit of that Lucky Strike purifying process, described by the words—"It's toasted". That's why folks in every city, town and hamlet say that Luckies are such mild cigarettes.

"It's toasted"
That package of **mild** Luckies

Though spectacular, "Nature in the Raw" did not rank with best. Eric the Red sailed into print in 1932.

During the depression Hill used some "reminder ads." Simple layouts like this appeared in 1933 and 1934.

Along with leaf storage sheds, stemmery and factory gave American a fully integrated cigarette center at Richmond. Today there are three other centers, each of similar size—Reidsville, Durham and Louisville.

appeared to be a shift of the nation's smoking habits. To his credit, however, he refused to be panicked into taking his eye off the ball, and met the problem in his characteristic head-on fashion.

Deflation

A realist, Hill was not thrown into despair by the decreased consumption of cigarettes at the standard price, $6.04 per thousand to wholesalers: after all, there was less money to be spent on every commodity. But he was determined not to let the curve of cigarette consumption drop. In 1933, American Tobacco cut its price to $4.85 a thousand.

In the midst of this price upheaval there were other developments. The standard cigarette package was greatly improved by a wrapping of moisture-proof cellophane, which kept the contents fresher longer. And Hill went the trend one better with the addition of the Lucky Tab for quick opening. But this advance

unprofitable item, Hill might well have been tempted to get back into the briar pipe business and ride what

White building at Blackwell and Pettigrew Streets, Durham, was built by the old Blackwell Company as a Bull Durham factory. It now houses headquarters for Durham branch and for American Suppliers, Inc.

In 1931 Charles Neiley took charge of all manufacture and leaf buying. A bear for detail, Neiley supervised cigar making, handled his own labor relations as well.

The same year a young lawyer named Paul Hahn joined American Tobacco, did administration, advertising, public relations. Vincent Riggio (right), a veteran of the Butler-Butler days, was sales Vice President.

was almost overlooked in the price-conscious mood of the day; the No. 2 cigarette company advertised the new wrap heavily without a flicker of sales response, and the makers of some cigarettes advertised gleefully "you can't smoke cellophane."

Falling leaf prices were not as gleefully regarded in the tobacco patch. They reflected bitter, biting hardship among the thousands of small farmers for whom the golden weed was, just as in colonial days, the money crop. President Hoover asked for help in mid-1931 and Hill announced: "Without regard to price and without regard to what any other tobacco company may do, The American Tobacco Company will commit itself to buy from 12% to 14% more poundage in 1931 than it bought in 1930." A minimum average purchasing price was also stipulated, and the arrangement repeated in later years. Throughout the emergency the Company did better than its promise, as to both quantity and price.

Despite some consumers' apparent indifference to the quality of what they smoked, Hill hewed to the line that had begun in 1917. "Sunshine Mellows, Heat Purifies"; "Consider Your Adam's Apple"; "Nature in the Raw is Seldom Mild" were among the new themes.

New ideas were not limited to the advertising department—which, in effect, consisted of George Hill and Lasker. In 1929 Charles F. Neiley was made Vice President, and emerged from C. A. Penn's shadow as a key figure in the modern Company. He was a remarkably versatile man in an organization run by all-round executives rather than specialists. At various times Neiley had been corporate Secretary, leaf buyer and factory man. He is remembered as a "detail hound," but one who was really loved. It was natural that Neiley should handle labor relations (he personally negotiated with the unions, a tradition followed by Vice Presidents Fowler and Crowe) in addition to running the factories. In 1931, after Penn's death, Neiley was given charge of leaf buying also, with Jim Lipscomb reporting to him. The Richmond constellation of plants was completed about the time of Neiley's accession, carrying out the idea that each major location should be a complete unit in itself, embracing leaf storage, stemming and manufacture.

The year of *Lucky Strike*'s emergence as top

brand, 1931, saw an unusual departure in management practise. A young lawyer with the Company's attorneys had attracted the officers' attention for his alertness and knowledge of the tobacco business. They decided to bring him into the Company as a director and Assistant to the President, a title that was changed to Vice President inside of a year. Almost from the first, Paul Hahn was a "policy man," supervising the Company's public relations as well as its legal affairs and figuring prominently in sales and advertising planning. It was Hahn who handled the annual meeting of stockholders in Hill's absence.

New-fashioned salesman

Quiet, and as slight in build as Hill was big, Vincent Riggio was introducing new concepts of selling. He also put into effect Hill's "formula" for placing advertising materials in retail stores: at eye-level and either near a moving object, in a strong light, or in an aisle. Riggio was in the car with George Hill the day two women, one stout and one slim, inspired the "Reach for a *Lucky*" idea. His knee was the one Hill slapped in the first enthusiasm of discovery; but the sales chief was not too quiet when Hill's copy themes seemed too extreme. Riggio, who had been born in Sicily and was a tailor's assistant while Hill was attending Williams College, told Hill to his face that "Nature in the Raw" was a poor idea. And he may have been right: sales dropped seven billion units in 1932, although depression and the ten centers had a good deal to do with the drop in all three of the standard brands.

The new notions Riggio brought to the trade revolved around treatment of the dealer. He would rather lose a sale or two than load a tobacconist with an oversupply that would lead to selling dried-out cigarettes. He was able to temper the old-fashioned drummer's "get-the-order" philosophy with a regard for the Company's reputation that amounted almost to a sixth sense, now called "public relations."

In center leaves, no sand

During the lean years of the thirties, the national mood was quite different from that of the Roaring Twenties, the "Era of Wonderful Nonsense." So was Hill's. In cooperation with Riggio, he worked out a number of quality themes that lent themselves

"*Spinning Jinny*" demonstrated the selling principle of demonstration. The smaller cogwheel represented direct sales contact, the larger one, advertising.

"*Center leaves*" advertising in 1934-35-36 was tied in with one of Lucky Strike's most successful sales demonstrations. Taken apart and shaken out, a Lucky yields no sand, one indication of leaf types used.

Prominent in the Company's radio programs during the late thirties was Eddie Duchin. Though a virtuoso of classical stripe, Duchin preferred popular music.

"This is the old maestro, Ben Bernie and all the lads —yowsah," was familiar signoff on Company's radio offerings during the same era. Bernie, seldom without a cigar, was a talented band leader and comedian too.

more to demonstration than excitation: "Center Leaves," "Cream of the Crop," "A Light Smoke," "With Men who Know Tobacco Best, it's *Luckies* 2 to 1." As early as 1917, the Company's salesmen had carried a little set of pans in which to toast *Lucky Strike* tobacco. Late in 1926, a year after George Hill succeeded his father in the President's chair, a permanent exhibit was set up in a New York store, on Broadway near 45th Street. Passing pedestrians could look in on a cigarette machine actually rolling and packing *Lucky Strikes*. Legally, the "store" was a registered tobacco factory, subject to federal inspection; its Broadway run lasted almost five years. In 1934 came the "sand demonstration." Two cigarettes, one a *Lucky* and one a competing brand, were taken apart over a slip of white paper. The lack of sand and sediment under the dismantled *Lucky* demonstrated the use of "Clean Center Leaves" with a vividness no advertisement could match. The same procedure made it possible for the customer to observe the long strands of leaf in the *Lucky* blend, a feature which is still apparent in the brand's "tear and compare" demonstration. Toward the end of the decade salesmen were equipped with phonographs and even with a motion picture projector which combined the *Lucky Strike* "commercial" with filmed entertainment.

Although Hill regarded each successful demonstration as a small cog which would set a bigger word-of-mouth wheel in motion,* there was a distinct limit on the number of people one salesman could talk to on a given day. Furthermore the number of salesmen was shrinking—from 1,000 or so when George Hill took over to about half that number ten years later. The one-word reason: radio.

On the air

In broadcasting as in print media, Hill himself was a kind of one-man ad agency. And his concentration on national advertising even to the exclusion of salesmen paid off in volume. His first network show came in 1928, radio having graduated from the crystal-set-and-earphones stage. The *Lucky Strike* Radio

---

*Hill actually demonstrated this theory of demonstration with a small wheel meshed to a larger one. The gadget was duplicated by the dozen and issued to members of the sales force.

Hour (which evolved into Your Hit Parade) consisted simply of the most popular tunes played in a rhythmic beat with a minimum of cadenzas and "arranging." Among the commercials which interspersed the hit tunes that first year was "Reach for a *Lucky* Instead of a Sweet." Hill insisted the tunes be played just as people ordinarily heard them, feeling that the familiar context would help his commercials get across. They did. Critics objected to his tempi and his fortissimos, but people listened and smoked *Lucky Strike*. Although Hill was known as a big spender in the advertising world, he spent far less on advertising per thousand cigarettes sold than the industry average (a fact, incidentally, which has held true up to and including 1953).

Hill's career as a radio impresario included the Metropolitan Opera, the Hit Parade, Ben Bernie, Kay Kyser, Eddie Duchin, Jack Benny, Phil Harris, Wayne King and even columnist Dorothy Thompson. In 1937, Hill contracted with Warner Brothers for the radio appearance of any or all of its movie stars. "Your Hollywood Parade," heard on Wednesdays while "Hit Parade" broadcast on Saturdays, presented dozens of luminaries from the world of celluloid. And during the 1938-39 season Sophie Tucker, "last of the red hot mommas," did a stint for *Roi-Tan* cigars.

Off the ant hill

Hill probably thought more, and certainly said more, about the theory of advertising than any of his contemporaries. In 1929, he had mused:

> . . . only in bursts of subconscious enlightenment do we detach ourselves from what we want long enough to realize that the customer's vision of what he wants . . . is the only thing that differentiates us from the simple economy of the ant hill, where competition has been obliterated . . . competition therefore reduces itself to the field of human consciousness.

Ten years later he had tempered this mystic view to include the role of manufacturing:

> Now all the "hot air," the "bunk" and the "hooey" in the world won't make Mr. Consumer buy the second time if he is not satisfied with his first purchase. So the wise advertiser must speak truthfully of the merit of his product . . . no one in the tobacco business makes a profit on an initial sale. It's the repeat business that pays dividends, therefore, the

Sophie Tucker was among the Broadway and Hollywood luminaries who advertised American Tobacco products during the thirties. Others included such popular orchestra leaders as Phil Harris and Wayne King.

Early career of Frank Sinatra included appearances on the Lucky Strike Hit Parade. First of a new kind of crooner, Sinatra was soon dubbed a "teensation."

importance of "quality of product," the importance of pleasing the consumer so that he will return to make the repeat purchase.

In 1938 Hill received his most treasured testimonial almost accidentally. A business professor of the Harvard Graduate School was assigned to study the tobacco industry, and after a visit to the Richmond factory spelled out his impressions:

> I was truly amazed at the constant and relentless emphasis on quality. Tremendous expense in equipment and costly processing treatments were apparently being undertaken to give every assurance to the smoker that when he smokes a *Lucky Strike* he should never be aware of the slightest variation in quality. It was surprising, because as a layman and a somewhat indifferent smoker I had never realized the enormous effort and expense devoted to quality in a cigarette.

The good fight

The Cigarette Ferris Wheel, as the standard brand battle was called, continued to revolve. With Hill drumming the radio beat and sloganizing the printed copy, it was by far advertising's most spirited contest—in magazine pages, in newspapers, on radio, via point-of-sale pieces and rural billboards. Except that the new dimension of television has been added, it is waged with equal fervor today. "A good fight," said Hill in 1941, "helps everybody."

He was correct, but the fight that helped most was not the kind of fight he had in mind. Cigarette consumption did not climb sensationally during the thirties, and *Lucky Strike* sales finished 1940 just about at the level of 1930. But all three big brands profited greatly from the War II stimulus, each moving up from the 35-45,000,000,000 range to a 55-70,-000,000,000 zone in 1945. Following that year *Lucky Strike* and *Camel* broke out of the trio to a 1948 peak around the hundred billion level.

When Hill's twenty-one-year tenure ended, the Ferris Wheel had put him on top more often than not. *Lucky Strike* was number one in twelve of the twenty-one years, number two in five years, number three in four. But well before Hill's career ended, and even before War II clamped down on experimentation, a new influence came on. The war was to cloud its importance for a while, but in the end the new factor was to add a new dimension—literally and figuratively—to cigarette competition.

MODERN DESIGN

NO ONE can say when Americans first became conscious of "modern" design. Europe was first with the glass wall, the apartment house on stilts, the clean and uncluttered line. In this country, teardrop contours were tried on automobiles—unsuccessfully— as early as 1933. But it is safe to say that the New York World's Fair of 1939 brought the trend to a focus: the long, low building silhouette; the stark, undecorated façade; the "functional look."

American Tobacco's structure at the Fair was as modern as the rest. In a setting of picture windows, simple planes and dioramas showing how tobacco is grown and manufactured was a real production line. After sniffing a trayful of blended and shredded tobacco, spectators saw it pass through making and packing machines to emerge as cartons of *Lucky Strike* cigarettes. Toward the Fair's close in 1940, there was something modern around each score of smokes: Raymond Loewy redesigned the green package, cleaning up the lettering and putting the red bull's-eye trademark on both front and back.*

The new awareness of design, interrupted by War II, was to result in the ranch house, the stream-lined electric iron, the chair that crouched like a spider and the automobile resembling a bullet with false teeth. But all this was foreshadowed, in a way, by the everyday cigarette. And the cigarette by then *was* an everyday item—on the average, every American of smoking age used about five each day. It was an accepted accessory of the up-to-date citizen. President Franklin D. Roosevelt, a pipe smoker during the early twenties, now sported a cigarette in a long holder. Perhaps this had some cosmic connection with "modern design" in smoking—the king-sized cigarette.

The La Corona of cigarettes

In any event, 1939 saw the conversion of *Pall Mall* to the eighty-five millimeter length,* about a fifth longer than the standard seventy millimeter cigarette. It caught on fast. In spite of the ensuing war, which actually eliminated *Pall Mall* advertising for a time, the sales curve climbed more steeply than any major brand before or since. The reasons? Mildness had something to do with it: tobacco is its own

---

*Some years later Loewy also took a look at the *Pall Mall* package, reported he could see no way to improve it.

*The length and circumference were indirectly limited by the tax statutes, which define "small cigarettes" as those weighing not more than three pounds per thousand. Above that weight the excise tax increases.

World's Fair of 1939 on Flushing meadows included a Lucky Strike building. Inside, machines rolled and wrapped tobacco into finished packs of Luckies. In 1940 the average adult smoked five cigarettes a day.

best filter and the longer unsmoked butt of the longer cigarette was just that. Package design doubtless helped too—the brilliant *Pall Mall* red was the first "decorator color" to surround a big brand. And the shape of the cigarette itself made a difference, for long and slender were by now synonyms for "fashionable." Women particularly liked the new length at first, although men took it up too, just as they were taking up longer, thinner Corona and Panatela cigars (newest shape in the *La Corona* line, for instance, is a longer and thinner version of the Corona shape, the "Rajah").

For thirty years after the Company bought *Pall Mall* along with Butler-Butler, that brand name had been attached to extra-special (and extra-expensive) Turkish cigarettes. By the early thirties, there were fully thirteen different sizes and shapes of *Pall Mall*, boxed in the distinctive red and crested in gold. In 1936 it was brought out as a "modern blend" with

less Turkish leaf and no flavoring. In a sense, this was a throwback to the days before the Burley blends; the new domestic cigarette was put up in the regular "cup package" and priced with the standards. In this form it did a reasonably good business, reaching an annual rate close to 600,000,000 units by the year of the World's Fair. At this point the "modern blend" was made a flavored Burley mixture; the standard length gave way to "modern design." To give it separate sales and advertising attention, *Pall Mall* had been leased to the American Cigarette and Cigar subsidiary (the old American Cigar Company, renamed in 1936), which was headed by Albert Gregg. The first advertising of the present blend began late in 1939; early in 1940 Paul Hahn took over as president of Cigarette and Cigar.

From the first, the Long Reds were "class" cigarettes. They were introduced with great dignity, and great expense, by direct sampling on silver salvers at 497 of the nation's finest hotels. And the four-color advertisements which in 1940 followed up this top-level debut were models of distinguished design in keeping with the "longer, more distinguished cigarette."

Paul Hahn and Pall Mall

It was Hahn who masterminded the mass promotion. His clinching campaign for *Pall Mall* was tuned as closely to the public consciousness, perhaps, as any advertising can be. "Modern design makes the big difference" was the tag line, and apt illustrations were provided by the progress of rearmament. Modern design in tanks, rifles and aircraft was compared to the cigarette's new shape; so successful were the ads themselves that billboard copies of them were being used in China ten years afterward—with the name *Pall Mall* blotted out and any one of a number of commodities substituted! As war came closer, another historic campaign emphasized the military theme via radio "spot commercials" of a minute or less. "On the land, in the air and on the sea," punctuated by the rising beep, *beep*, BEEP of a destroyer whistle went on the air 4,490 times a week. The war sidetracked this campaign for the duration—among other things, the war mobilizers thought the triple beep might be taken for an air-raid warning. Later, problems of securing distribution in a topsy-turvy market—not to mention leaf and people—put *Pall Mall* advertising temporarily on the shelf.

Nevertheless, the 1940 drive had doubled *Pall Mall* sales in a year and brought a flock of imitations to the market. Even in his preoccupation with *Lucky Strike*, George Hill was impressed. That same year the parent company converted *Herbert Tareyton* to "modern size," although the brand had been doing well—close to a billion unit sales in 1938 and 1939.

Tareyton had a peripatetic past, both as a cigarette and as a high grade pipe tobacco (the latter still sold by the Company). The name referred to no actual person: *Herbert* had been plucked out of the air by the Falk Tobacco Company of Richmond and New York, registered as a cigarette trademark in 1913. The cigarette started life as a "drop shipment brand" with the Falk Tobacco Company, which was then a pipe tobacco house specializing in high-grade and private brands. Among its products were *Serene*,

The rich aroma of tobacco "in sweet case"—once reserved for cigarette makers—was one attraction for visitors to the Lucky Strike exhibit at the Fair.

Radio celebrities included L. A. "Speed" Riggs, the fast-talking auctioneer who chanted "Sold American!", and Lanny Ross, one of the Hit Parade's singing stars.

Other visitors included James Kyser, better known as Kay, and Ginny Sims. Her songs and his College of Musical Knowledge advertised Lucky Strike on radio.

Something is happening in the cigarette business!

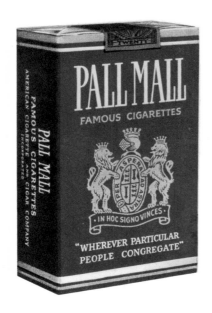

Look around—America.

Look in the Service. Look wherever you see young people. Something is happening in the cigarette business. A basic improvement in cigarette design is here.

It's Pall Mall—modern, streamlined,—over 20 per cent longer than your old cigarette,—designed for better smoking.

See what this step-forward in cigarette design does for you!

It is a scientific fact that tobacco is its own true filter. In Pall Mall the additional length travels the smoke further—giving you not alone a longer cigarette but a better cigarette—a definitely milder, a definitely cooler smoke.

Pall Mall is a smoother cigarette, too. BULKING—that natural process revived by Pall Mall—lets time do what machines can only approximate. BULKING causes the traditionally fine tobaccos of Pall Mall to mellow, softens all traces of harshness. As a result, Pall Mall is a really smoother smoke.

Prove it—yourself, try Pall Mall critically. See if you don't agree with millions that something is happening in the cigarette business!

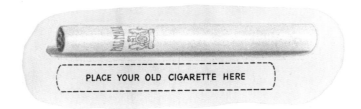

PLACE YOUR OLD CIGARETTE HERE

"WHEREVER PARTICULAR PEOPLE CONGREGATE"

90

London Sherbert and *Manhattan Cocktail* tobacco mixtures, with *Herbert Tareyton, Vaporia, Radiana* and *Johnny Walker* in a higher price bracket. To push these blends with retailers, Albert Falk made up *Herbert Tareyton* cigarettes to be sent to retailers as a kind of premium. It was not until one delighted jobber sent in an order for 25,000 that Falk even put a price on the new product. Like the best of his pipe tobaccos, *Tareyton* contained Latakia tobacco. Whether this feature appealed to pipe smokers or whether it was other ingredients in the blend, there was something about them smokers liked. (The carton still bears the phrase, "There's something about them you'll like.") At any rate, the brand was far too good to remain a premium very long; before Falk put a price on *Tareyton*, dealers were selling it at 25c for 20, a high figure for the days before War I.

Leased from Tobacco Products in 1923, *Tareyton* was farmed out to Union Tobacco in George Hill's first year as President. But it returned to American Tobacco in 1930 when Union was unable to pay the rental fee. *Tareyton's* blend was the kind favored by British smokers—mostly Bright tobacco, with no flavoring. Its 10% seasoning of Latakia was originally unique, and provoked imitation by at least two major brands. The monocled "Dude" was a symbol of its British blend and the genuine cork tip was unusual for a popular cigarette. While a specialty cigarette, its market was limited; like the special Turkish blends of the old *Pall Mall*, it was a kind of carryover from the early days. In fact, *Herbert Tareyton* cigarettes were the last to include premiums in the pack—three-dimensional fold-outs of English cathedrals and castles, lithographed in color. When the product and its pack were lengthened in 1940, the enveloped inserts disappeared. But late in the twenties *Tareyton* had been given a mixture of the same family as the *Lucky Strike* and the new *Pall Mall* blends. This, together with its elegant, cork-tipped length, made *Tareyton Pall Mall's* chief king-size competitor, a position it still holds.

Battle of Lexington

Along with new designs for living, the prewar years brought newly-designed interpretations of the old Sherman Antitrust Act. In 1940 the Justice Department began an action against the eight largest

Something was happening in the cigarette business, as the 1939 Pall Mall ad on the opposite page made clear. Modern design—meaning the king size—was beginning to make a big difference to smokers. So successful was the kinged Pall Mall that in 1940 Herbert Tareyton was also made 85 millimeters long.

In 1920 Franklin D. Roosevelt, Assistant Secretary of the Navy, smoked a pipe. Twenty-two years later he had switched to a "long" cigarette, symbolizing the gradual revolution in America's smoking habits.

tobacco manufacturers, claiming "conspiracy or combination in restraint of trade." There was no direct evidence of collusion. Government attorneys stressed that uniformity of leaf and product prices were the equivalent of a kind of tacit agreement not to indulge in price competition. This was the new concept of "conscious parallel action."

The trial took place in Lexington, Kentucky, the three largest companies defending, the others agreeing with the prosecution to abide by the result. The point at issue was "oligopolistic" control as distinct from monopolistic control in 1911. The tobacco companies pointed out that uniformity of prices, not only in products sold but also in leaf bought, could be explained as readily by competition as by "combination." The nickel candy bar and various other items of standard price were cited as evidence that simple supply and demand led inevitably to uniform policies in pricing and in other aspects of doing business. For five months during the summer and fall of 1941, the defense counsel for American, headed by George Whiteside, analyzed activities on the leaf and finished-product markets in terms of economic competition. The Government insisted that the identity in leaf and finished-product prices were circumstantial evidence of conspiratorial action. The verdict, which had to be based on circumstantial evidence in the absence of any indication of direct collusion, went against the industry.

The results of what is now called "the second battle of Lexington" were overlooked by the public in the excitement of the times, since the District Court's ruling came four days after Pearl Harbor. In any case, the precise reforms in industry practise desired by the Government were difficult to establish, let alone describe. Wrote Yale professor Richard Tennant in 1951:

> . . . the objectives of public policy are not entirely clear. If the law condemns market structure, does it condemn structure for its own sake or for certain undesirable results which are supposed to follow? . . . It is difficult to make a strong case for reform in the structure of the cigarette industry on noneconomic grounds alone . . . Although the law condemns size and concentrated power . . . it does not appear that the cigarette firms are large enough or powerful enough to be a suitable object of attack on these grounds alone . . . there is no

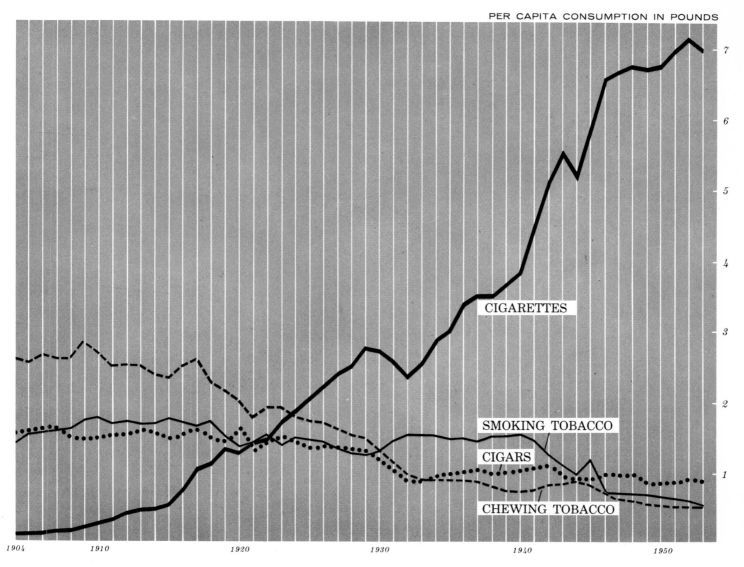

CIGARETTES

SMOKING TOBACCO

CIGARS

CHEWING TOBACCO

1904   1910   1920   1930   1940   1950

First fifty years of the new American Tobacco have seen both kinds of manufactured tobacco—chewing and smoking—fade in popularity as cigarettes grew phenomenally. Steepest cigarette increase has come during the last ten years. Sudden 1945 spurt in use of smoking tobacco (light line) was largely due to shortage of cigarettes. Although consumption of all cigars is down, purchases of fine cigars are higher. Snuff is omitted from graph, since its consumption is too small to show up clearly on this scale. All plots represent per capita consumption in pounds of unstemmed tobacco. Heavy line represents the use of cigarettes, dotted line cigars, broken line chewing tobacco and light line the use of smoking tobacco.

occasion for renewed major surgery on the structure of the industry. ("The American Cigarette Industry," Yale University Press.)

In explaining this structure with respect to price, George Washington Hill testified that "a slight differential in price was possible as between trade-mark brands" but "a large differential was practically, or was actually impossible unless a man wanted to sacrifice his business." And "only one consideration—that our business is built on the basis of service to the consumer—leads us to wish our products be sold no higher than competing brands." It could have been a classical economist speaking, for Hill was expressing the basic idea from which the cigarette industry—and every other competitive industry based on mass production—has grown. And it required considerable study by the industry's lawyers to devise ways in which tobacco companies could change some of their practises and thus show their willingness to conform to the decision. Nor could the leading analysts of the press make any suggestions. Concluded Time Magazine, scratching its puzzled

LUCKY STRIKE **GREEN** HAS GONE TO WAR!

So here's the smart new uniform for fine tobacco

Elimination of green from the Lucky Strike pack led to 1942's most dramatic advertising line, used only over the radio and on these carton inserts. Enough copper was saved in a year to provide bronze for 400 light tanks. Hill's ad was a lucky stroke indeed—it broke just as North Africa was invaded.

editorial head: " . . . nobody had any notion of how else the cigaret industry could or should operate."

After Lexington, the country and the Company faced more tangible problems in Europe and in the Pacific. In an Executive Order President Roosevelt listed tobacco as an essential food, and local draft boards were directed to defer tobacco farmers to insure continued output. Civilian smokers struggled with allocations while their favorite brands were shipped overseas by the billion. (Between 1940 and 1946, *Lucky* sales zoomed from 42,000,000,000 to 103,000,000,000, most of the increase going abroad.)

Short green

Competition, though, did not abate. In 1942, year of Roosevelt's Executive Order, a chlorophyll promoter suggested all cigarettes be treated with his product. The green stuff, said he, would protect the tobacco. But it was the elimination of green—the green on the *Lucky Strike* package—that made the year's big advertising story. The "*Lucky Strike* Green Has Gone to War" campaign broke very close to the North African invasion of 1942; in six weeks sales of the brand increased 38%.

This was one advertising campaign that originated in the Purchasing Department, headed since 1926 by Richard J. Boylan, who had started with the Company in 1900 as a knee-panted office boy. Early in 1942 Boylan told Hill that the gold panels on the *Lucky Strike* pack would have to go: the ink base was copper powder, and copper was way up on the critical list. Purchasing had gotten government approval to use some discarded gold ink, but somewhere

the ink had picked up an odor and was useless for American Tobacco's purposes. Soon afterward chromium, essential to the solid green used on *Lucky* labels, began to run low; Boylan had only a three months' supply of green ink when he approached Hill again. In his folder were substitute labels—red on black, red on gray, red on pastel green. "Is this the best you can do?" asked Hill. Boylan shrugged: "Just like the soldiers, green ink has gone to war." Hill's palm hit his glass-topped desk like a thunder-clap. For the next few days he pondered over the verbal possibilities, and "*Lucky Strike* Green Has Gone to War" was the result. Some commercials heard on the "Information Please" radio program consisted of those seven words repeated over and over again.

The late thirties had witnessed another supply save that turned out to be crucial. During War I, odorless cigarette paper was hard to find and after the Armistice Percival Hill went to France and bought a paper mill, Société Anonyme des Papeteries de Mauduit. The mill eventually turned out more cigarette paper than American Tobacco could use, and Harry Straus, a cork salesman, was given the agency to sell the excess French paper. Around 1937, when the oncoming war could almost be smelled, Straus and others set about building paper plants in this country. Three of the Company's competitors put up capital for Straus' Ecusta Paper Company. American Tobacco backed a second company, Peter T. Schweitzer, Inc. The new American mills got into production just about the time Hitler overran France; American now buys from both. The old French Papeteries de Mauduit was sold in 1951.

The war brought other changes. The crest on *Pall Mall*'s package, traditionally gold, was changed to white. With manpower short, the new Long Reds went on allocation and in 1944 and 1945 *Pall Mall* advertising was eliminated. But the brand, in seventh place by 1943, had made its mark. Late that year George Hill wrote a letter to the Company's employees who were overseas with the military. "Attached hereto," the letter read, "you will kindly find two good old American dollar greenbacks, which I ask that you invest wherever you may be in the cigarette of your choice." Hill was careful to mention *Pall Mall* as well as his beloved *Lucky*—something that would have been unthinkable two years earlier.

Cats and courts-martial

Not only production but distribution as well posed a problem for the industry at war. Despite vast overseas shipments of the big brands, troops in the field often had to make do with the "over-night brands" inspired by the shortage. The Supreme Commander in Europe threatened to court-martial anyone caught pilfering cigarettes intended for the armies in Europe. As one of its contributions to the total effort, American began to load its cigarette cases four and five high in freight cars, although rail carload rates were based on three-high stacking. Five layers took up 112.5 inches of the standard 120-inch clearance— "You couldn't get a cat up there," recalls Traffic Director Thomas P. Connors. But the new loading saved one freight car out of three. And beginning in January, 1946, Connors got the railroads to discount the excess over-the-minimum weight to 80% of the regular carload rate. The rest of the industry, of course, benefited too from the new arrangement.

In 1944, as Operation Overlord was closing in against the Siegfried Line, Hill received a letter from the Army Service Forces depot at Jersey City. "Special commendation," it went, "is extended to your company for meritorious service rendered to our Armed Forces Overseas. It is a pleasure to collaborate with your organization in supplying American troops with *Lucky Strike* Cigarettes, *Half and Half* and *Blue Boar* Smoking Tobacco. Despite difficulties in obtaining packing materials, the mission assigned your organization has always been accomplished promptly . . . " *Lucky Strike* itself, as well as *Lucky Strike*

Ecusta paper mill in North Carolina's Pisgah Forest began production just before Nazis overran French plant, makes cellophane as well as cigarette paper.

Richard J. Boylan, who took charge of purchasing in 1926, now buys from 3,000 suppliers. His remark led Hill to phrase, "Lucky Strike Green Has Gone to War."

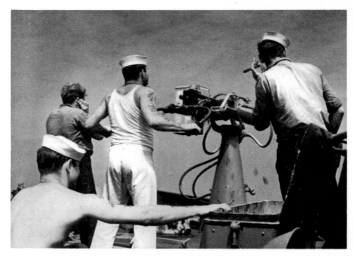

Even in combat tobacco was vital—to sailors as well as ground troops. Supreme Commander promised court-martial for those stealing soldiers' tobacco.

95

green, was going to war. In one year more than half the brand's volume, then approaching the 100,000,-000,000 level, went overseas for American troops. This was a vote of confidence from the nation's young men; but it pinched the civilian market considerably and led to the smoking of substitutes on the home front, a bleak happenstance for any brand manufacturer.

Still, production and financial difficulties were the same for all as leaf prices more than doubled between 1940 and 1946. The statistics suggest, in fact, a degree of brand loyalty that one would not have imagined feasible after a four-year pinch. When the troops streamed back home, smokers turned back to the standard brands in such numbers that the three largest increased their market share from 72% to 83% in two years. In 1946 alone, domestic sales of *Lucky Strike* increased by 32,000,000,000 – by far the greatest one-year increase in the history of tobacco. In that year the Company reflected more than ever the dogged, one-product concentration of G. W. Hill. Some 95% of its dollar sales – then $764 million – were contributed by cigarettes; and 95% of the cigarettes were *Lucky Strike*.

The pressure of wartime demand left an odd hangover in Europe, where cigarettes for a time took the place of money. Armed with a carton of American smokes, anyone could secure food, drink, lodging or clothing not only in bombed Berlin but in France, Italy and even Switzerland. The use of cigarettes for this purpose was later stopped at the source, by limiting postal shipments to the occupation troops from this country.

The blueprint

One thing the war did not stop was *Lucky Strike* advertising. Kay Kyser's College of Musical Knowledge continued every Wednesday night, virtually all his shows being given before soldier audiences at army camps. The Hit Parade on Saturday turned up a new "teensation" named Frank Sinatra. He was not long, however, for the show world of G. W. Hill; his slow delivery and lazy syncopations did not fit the rhythmic drumbeat on which Hill still insisted.

In 1943 an Advertising Research Foundation survey named a *Lucky Strike* ad as one of the ten best-read in the nation's newspapers. Containing only six words – "Yes! *Lucky Strike Means Fine Tobacco*" – the ad pictured an overalled farmer rising from a field of tobacco. Since this was one of a number of tobacco-country paintings Hill had commissioned,

American Tobacco men who know tobacco best operate American Suppliers, domestic leaf-buying subsidiary. President James F. Strickland (left) makes his base in Bright region as does John R. Hutchings (center), a Vice President. Burley purchases are handled by Executive Vice President John S. Dowd of Louisville.

Tobacco farmer with golden leaf was painted by James Chapin, one of a series commissioned by George Hill.

"George's Genie" featured newspaper ad later named one of best-read by Advertising Research Foundation.

George W. Hill

the massive figure became known as "George's Genie." Around this time Hill's own son, George Washington Hill, Jr., had come into his own as a potent force in the Company's management. Though not the dramatic personality his father was, Hill, Jr., had gradually taken over most of the advertising supervision. He was instrumental in obtaining the "Information Please" program and did much to make the chant of the tobacco auctioneer part of the nation's stream of consciousness, along with the phrase, "Sold American!"

In 1945 the Saturday Evening Post surveyed ten years of cigarette sales and advertising and found that *Lucky Strike* had spent only $55.5 million in magazines, newspapers and radio time to sell 436,-

100,000,000 cigarettes. Over the same span, the Post figured, its two big rivals spent $85.9 and $84.2 million to sell 817,600,000,000 units between them. *Lucky*'s "traceable ad costs" were thus 12.7c per thousand, against 20.8c per thousand for the brand's two major competitors. Ever the showman, Hill had the charts and tables reproduced in white on dark blue and bound them into the 1945 annual report. This was the "blueprint" of his ten-year drive to the top.

The Post's advertising study was, in a sense, Hill's personal epitaph; the 1945 annual report, issued in the spring of 1946, was the last he signed. In September of the latter year Hill died at his Quebec fishing camp.

L.S./M.F.T.

VINCENT RIGGIO had always been a kind of balance wheel for G. W. Hill. It was somehow right that the job of charting a new and more balanced course should fall to the trim little salesman.

To begin with, the great gains racked up by *Lucky Strike* during the Second World War could be credited to the manufacturing department under Preston Fowler and John Crowe, rather than to inspired advertising. Any of the major manufacturers could have sold 50% more cigarettes on the home front, had the usual flow of materials been available. There were restrictions on sugar, on tinfoil, on glycerin (the hygroscopic agent which helps cigarette tobacco stay moist). A "lend-leaf" program was set up for the United Nations, since tobacco commerce outside the U. S. was seriously disrupted.* And the most crucial element of all—people—was also in short supply, as 3,067 of the Company's 18,815 employees marched off to the wars.

No department, no line of products was exempt. *Half and Half* had been endowed with a two-part tin can which telescoped as the tobacco was used up: the war killed it. And for a time, one of the big brands—*Herbert Tareyton*—was actually taken out of production.

American weathered all this. *Herbert Tareyton*, whose production suspension had lasted for several months, was put back on stream. But another shortage, not entirely born of war, soon became evident—in the sales force. Hill's reliance on advertising had literally decimated it, and the military draft had almost finished it off. As long as Hill continued his virtuoso verbalizing, the shortcoming was not apparent in the sales curve. But after he died, the lack was glaring.

V-R Day

Riggio's task, therefore, was a double one. A new sales army had to be recruited almost from scratch, a time-consuming task. Meanwhile, Riggio had to depend largely on advertising. The latter was easier said than done, for the battleground of brand rivalry had changed. Hill's greatest triumphs had been won during the twenties, when the public heart was young and gay. Company advertising during the thirties took on a changed tone as new competition and a more sober national mood ruled out "nature in the raw." Hill himself, the master showman, had sensed the difference. His next few efforts—"*Lucky for You, It's a Light Smoke!*", "*I'm Your Best*

---

*Between March 1941 and the end of 1945, $267 million worth of leaf was "loaned." This was a substantial poundage: in 1945 American Tobacco's leaf purchases totaled $145 million.

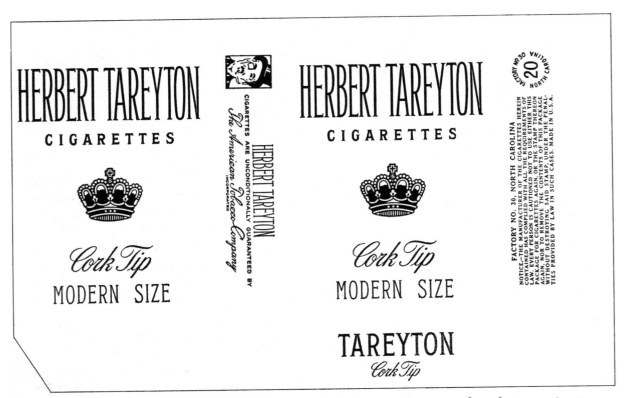

Until 1928 Tareyton was a Bright blend. Added Burley plus extra length spurred sales.

Friend," "Have You Tried a *Lucky* Lately?," "Better than Ever Tobacco Crops Plus Toasting Make *Luckies* Better than Ever"—were definitely milder. But in 1942 he turned out a phrase which delighted Riggio: "*Lucky Strike* Means Fine Tobacco." The sales chief frequently told Hill those five words would last longer than any other advertising the Company had coined. After a while, Hill came to share his feeling. In 1944 the phrase was well enough known to be reduced to "L.S./M.F.T." In his own broad pen-strokes Hill wrote out the initials and ordered them printed on the bottom of the white *Lucky* pack. They are still there, just as he wrote them.

In every year of Riggio's Presidency, which ended early in 1950, "L.S./M.F.T." was a prominent feature of his advertising. Among the other campaigns of his regime were "*Lucky Strike* Presents the Man Who Knows," "First Again with Tobacco Men," "Smoke a *Lucky* to Feel Your Level Best."

Losing business to the rising *Pall Mall* and *Herbert Tareyton*, sales of *Lucky Strike* receded from the 1946 peak. The sensational success of *Pall Mall* and "modern design" brought rivals into the king-size market, and the standard-size market as a whole began to decline. Once the new trend became estab-

lished, however, the downward direction of *Lucky Strike* sales began to seem less of a tragedy to the old-timers who had for many years put sweat and tears, if not blood, into that brand. And a vast segment of the public still recognized that "L.S./M.F.T." In 1953 it was second only to *Camel* and in that year, which saw the standard-size market shrink by nearly 15%, domestic sales of *Lucky Strike* dipped only 9%.

Original Tareyton design included crown but lacked Dude, was registered by Falk Tobacco Company in 1913.

Once straight Turkish, Pall Mall was "domesticated" in 1936, given cased Burley in 1939.

While the Company's own twin kings chipped away at sales of standard-length cigarettes, including *Lucky*, American's share of all cigarette sales increased from 29.6% at war's end to 32.6% in 1953. It was, and is, impractical to add "P.M./M.F.T." and "H.T./M.F.T." to the original *Lucky* leaf phrase. But it is significant that both *Pall Mall* and *Tareyton* are made of the same fine tobacco grades as *Lucky*, although they are blended differently. And it is also significant that since the 1890s American Tobacco has bought most of its own cigarette tobacco not through leaf dealers but direct from the farmer on the loose-leaf auctions.

The matter of leaf

The importance of this fact requires some reference to the history of tobacco itself, for the plant grows in a vast and variegated number of grades. The tobacco Rolfe first found in the Virginia tidelands was *Nicotiana rustica*, a dark coarse plant with a very high nicotine content. This was "uppowoc." To get a smokable leaf, the early Virginians imported seed from the Spanish possessions; Trinidad or Orinoco leaf was the *Nicotiana tabacum* species that aroused Europe to enthusiasm, via Portugal and Jean Nicot.

But merely importing the new species did not guarantee the growth of so-called "sweet-scented" tobacco. (The best results were to come later from a shift to sandy, poorer soil.) The "best" was defined by the market, at that time Europe: smokers themselves discovered that bright leaf was the sweetest, and "fancy yellow" brought premium prices a century before the Revolution. But its production was accidental: after 1750 much tobacco was fire-cured, and the smoke itself has a discoloring effect. Not until shortly before the Civil War was a flue-curing appara-

Original Pall Mall was boxed, came in several sizes. Banquet size was, and is, 92 mm—longer than kings.

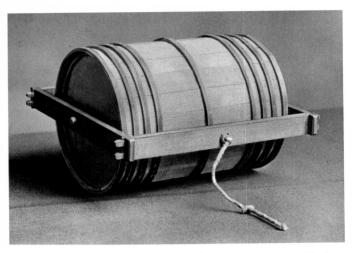

Coarse "shipping leaf" of 17th century was rolled to market in the hogshead. In mid-1800s, fine-textured cigarette leaf came into demand and forced a change.

Hogshead sales made quality purchasing a problem. It was difficult to sample a hogshead, easy to "nest" tobacco, i.e., conceal trash inside fine outer layer.

During vogue for manufactured tobacco, sales by the hogshead were the rule, as in Louisville, above. Much leaf was sweetened, had to be tough to make "chaw."

tus worked out which would "starve" the darkness out of the leaf without "smoking" it.

Too, the earlier method of transporting tobacco militated against the Bright. The planter packed his rough leaf into hogsheads which were drawn like wheels along the dirt trails, spikes being driven into the ends to serve as axles. These paths, or rather ruts, came to be known as "tobacco roads." Under such treatment, the fine leaf of today would probably end up as snuff.

The Slades of Caswell

Rustic experiments with charcoal, with primitive flues and with steam heat went on, all three being means to avoid "smoking" the leaf dark. Around 1825 the only yellow leaf of note was grown in Maryland and Ohio. Then, around 1838, the Slade brothers, whose farm was just below the Virginia-Carolina line south of Danville, solved the problem. Three factors were necessary to grow thin-leaved Bright tobacco: (1) light, porous soil, (2) some way to apply constant heat to the leaf without smoke, and (3) heat-tight curing barns which could be ventilated at will. The last was important; toward the end of the cure the moisture driven out of the green leaves must be gotten out of the barn lest it condense on the half-dry tobacco and stain it. The new method was risky. To get the lemon coloring great heat was needed, and a hotted-up barn full of dry leaves was a good tinder box for any stray spark (and still is). Nor could soil be selected for Bright cultivation just by looking at it. A given acre could yield leaf of a fine light color and flavor, while land across the road might grow nothing better than "shipping leaf."

When word of the Slades' bonanza crop got around, the piedmont took up tobacco cultivation. The reason? Most of the soil was useless for anything else. North Carolina, "the land of tar, pitch and pork," was mostly a piney desert sparsely populated. Tobacco changed everything. Ten years before the Civil War, Caswell County land was selling at $25 per acre (it went for a couple of dollars in the pre-Slade days). Durham Station metamorphosed from a whistle stop into a thriving town devoted to tobacco manufacture, and the influx of Sherman's blue troops and Johnston's grays in 1865 did the rest. At the same time Richmond began to lose out as a tobacco town: Libby Prison itself was originally a tobacco factory which had been sold to a ship-chandler just before Sumter.

Gold leaf and white

As Old Belt planters rushed to buy flues and get in on "gold leaf" prices, selling in hogsheads gave way to the loose-leaf auction.* Prizing (pressing tobacco into hogsheads) tended to injure the most delicate leaves, which came into demand first as plug wrappers, then as "cutters" suitable for shredding into cigarettes. Besides, manufacturers developed greater consciousness of grade, and proper sorting of top and center leaves, lugs and primings was facilitated by loose-leaf selling. As the cigarette brands with their special needs grew, grading became even more important. And as King Cotton was dethroned and "fi-cent cotton" appeared, tobacco cultivation spread to the coastal area of North Carolina (the "new belt") and into South Carolina. The panic of 1893, which drove cotton down to 4.6c, accelerated the changeover. Virginia, long accustomed to fire-curing, was somewhat slower in turning to Bright leaf. By 1918, Bright farming began in Georgia and Florida, but even today the great bulk of "bright canary yellow" is grown in North Carolina.

The second great development in tobacco, Burley, was more of a happenstance than the long and tortured evolution of Bright. Along the bottom lands near the Ohio River as along the tidewater of colonial Virginia, Kentuckians and Ohioans had taken up the cultivation of dark, fire-cured leaf. The "breaks" centered in Cincinnati, from which town hogsheads could be shipped by water to the New Orleans wharves. In 1864, a new variety was discovered in Ohio; its leaf had little or no sugar content and could absorb great quantities of sweet liquids. It was thus ideal for the makers of navy, or sweet, plug. Since it was also lighter-bodied and milder, the new type later modified the cigarette with the astounding volume results already described.

All White Burley, which is really a warm light brown, is said to be descended from the seed of a single plant. The original plant seems to have been

---

*The new auctions continued to be called "breaks," a term derived from breaking open the hogsheads for the buyer's inspection.

Surrender of Johnston's Confederate Army to Sherman took place near Durham. While awaiting terms, troops had chance to sample the new flue-cured Bright leaf.

Fame of Durham tobacco spread around the world after war ended. Thomas Carlyle, famous British historian, smoked Bull Durham tobacco through a "yard of clay."

Prizing tobacco on the farm tended to injure finely-textured leaves. These came into favor first as plug wrappers and later as "cutters" for cigarette use.

Bright leaf is produced in North Carolina, Virginia, South Carolina, Georgia and Florida. High in sugar content, it is the main ingredient in all big brands.

Burley tobacco grows in Kentucky and in Tennessee. Lacking sugar, it readily absorbs flavoring, is ideal for sweet plug, smoking tobacco, cigarettes.

a mutation or "sport," a biological accident. Burley soon displaced the former dark leaf in Kentucky, helped along by the fact that it was air-cured (*i.e.*, hung up to dry) instead of fire-cured.

Circuit riders vs. pinhookers

Almost from the founding of American Tobacco in 1890, much of the Company's leaf was purchased by its own buyers, whose traveling supervisors are still called "circuit riders." Beginning during the nineties, buyers went from town to town and even from farm to farm, buying the Company's tobacco direct from growers. Although American Tobacco's management has run more to all-around

executives than to specialists, the leaf men remain a race unto themselves. They constitute a separate leaf-buying subsidiary, American Suppliers. It takes five years training before a man can buy leaf on his own; recognizing the Company's requirements by feel and sight, and more often by sight alone, is an art. Oddly enough, the judgments of good leaf buyers as to nicotine content, sweetness and mildness preceded scientific analysis of leaf in the laboratory. In some respects the chemists only confirm what the leaf man already knows.

Duke's leaf buyers, who were more particular than exporters, had a good deal to do with the end of the hogshead break and the spread of loose-leaf

Turkish leaf is small, expensive and aromatic. Few big brands nowadays lack a seasoning of Turkish— 10% or less. Subsidiary buys American's needs direct.

Small amounts of Maryland tobacco are blended into cigarettes, contribute distinctive flavor. Air-cured and free-burning, it is still marketed in hogsheads.

Although soil is the most important item in raising fine tobacco, seed must be of proper strain and free of fungus spores. A tablespoonful plants six acres.

Before seeding, bed is hoed and burned over to rid soil of weed seeds and insect eggs. Then the earth is raked smooth and the seed sown early in spring.

buying from Danville west to Louisville, Cincinnati and Lexington. And they soon became a more important factor on the market than the export brokers. Perhaps naturally, farmers were more apt to damn Duke as the author of their ills than to credit him with providing an expanded market for their crops. The new loose-leaf buying ended "nesting"—packing good leaf around the outside of a hogshead and filling the center with trash. Loading the hands of tobacco with soil—"sanding"—was also largely eliminated. And direct purchase by the manufacturer did not sit well with the old time leaf speculator or "pinhooker." One of these small dealers, who skimmed profits by re-grading poorly classified tobacco or buying leaf on

the street from impatient growers, saw that the game was up and joined American Tobacco. He was John Blackwell Cobb, father-in-law of George Washington Hill, one of Duke's Vice Presidents during the nineties and later President of American Cigar.

Pools, prices and politics

But most tobacco speculators resented the big, new New York organization which was relegating them to the sidelines. Their resentment seems to have spread to some warehousemen and to the farmer himself. After peace was declared between American and the English Imperial Company in 1902, one Danville leaf man opined that competition between

To protect tiny seedlings from raw spring weather, the bed is covered with cheesecloth pegged to the border logs. Six-inch seedlings are transplanted.

Young tobacco plants are set out in rows three or four feet apart. Planting is usually done through a tapered chute which punches holes in soft ground.

Among the early loose-leaf warehouses was Parrish's in Durham. In 1884 it advertised sales of "nearly eight million pounds" the previous year, about one-third of North Carolina's total crop. There are more warehouses now, but few sell over eight million pounds.

In Kentucky, dispute between independent farmers and those who wanted to pool their leaf led to violence. The military was ordered out to quell "night riding."

the two giants would cease, and lower leaf prices would result. But the Danville average went from 7.94c a pound in 1903 to 8.55c, 9.42c, 9.11c and 11.42c in successive years, the last-named figure representing a seventeen-year high. Nevertheless, farmers in both Bright and Burley areas did not feel very friendly toward anybody: chewing leaf came into an over-supply, heavy rains spoiled an occasional crop, beetles attacked, Japanese buyers got their leaf from brokers' storage instead of from warehouse floors, and the panic of 1907 topped off their troubles.

The farmers' discontent was not, in truth, new. During the 1870s, the Granger movement had trained its guns on the warehousemen of Danville, but the Grange could not counteract poor crops as a cause of low prices and when the leaf market turned up in 1878, Grangering faded out. A decade later the Farmers' Alliance in the Bright Belt demanded that warehousemen eliminate some of the weighmen, salesmen, clerks and factotums who padded the spread between farmers' and manufacturers' prices. In 1887 the Alliancemen hit on the idea of cutting back the crop to force prices up. Next year Old Belt production went down slightly, but so did prices. Alliance warehouses were set up, but no extra efficiency was achieved, and the warehouse commission was not lowered.

The old Alliance evolved into the Tobacco Growers' Protective Association. Local politicians campaigned for office by "cussin' out" American Tobacco, counting on the farm vote to ride them into office. By 1909, however, the Bright tobacco pool had settled on a simple means of improving their lot: they redried their leaf and stored it for direct sale to the manufacturer. This outcome was most satisfactory on both sides. When James B. Duke returned to the piedmont from England at the outbreak of War I, he was nominally engaged in forming the Southern Power Company (later Duke Power). But he still indulged his old fondness for talking tobacco with farmers, and continued to encourage cooperative marketing. Among other things, Duke did not want to see more leaf grown than the world could smoke.

During the war to end wars, leaf prices sky-rocketed as high as 54c and in 1920 comparable grades fizzled to 22c or even less. New cooperatives, the Tri-State Tobacco Growers and the Burley Tobacco

First loose-leaf auctions, like this Winston sale, took place around 1900 in the Old Belt of central North Carolina. With cigarettes coming into their own, manufacturers found it necessary to pick and choose more and finer grades—a procedure which was impractical in buying tobacco by the hogshead.

Growers, were formed. American Tobacco explicitly told its leaf buyers that "This company is not antagonistic nor opposed to this idea if it can benefit the farmers and manufacturers." But after a few years, the pools evaporated. Leaf prices climbed out of the 1920 pit, suggesting to farmers that the co-ops might be unnecessary after all; the pools developed high-priced "managements" and did not seem to perform the grading function adequately; and the independent warehousemen refused to shut up shop. Fortunately for the future of the leaf market, the large manufacturers including American Tobacco had continued to buy on the auction sales as well as from the pools. American and Imperial, the largest buyers, were accused of boycotting the latter, but the Federal Trade Commission dismissed the charge as groundless.

Barn for curing "fancy yellow" (Bright) leaf evolved during 19th century. Essential were flues to spread heat without smoke, ventilators to let out moisture.

Calvin Coolidge, a farmer himself, opposed bill to support farm prices. He feared one-crop farming and exhaustion of the soil would be the ultimate result.

107

Tobacco thrives under the blinding sun of midsummer. Too much rainfall weakens and thins out the leaves. Farmers weed the rows constantly, hope against hail.

Flowers are nipped in the bud to divert all of the plant's energy into the leaves. Deflowered plants send out suckers which are cut for the same reason.

"There ought to be a law. . . "

By 1925 the pools had ceased to hold the interest of tobacco planters, who were now looking toward Washington. In 1924 the first McNary-Haugen bill was introduced, calling for a government-financed export corporation. This would buy up farm surpluses so as to keep a constant ratio between agricultural prices and the general industrial index. But tobacco growers did not take kindly to "export dumping," and farmers generally were mixed in their reactions. In 1927 a fourth version of McNary-Haugen was passed in the Congress but vetoed by President Coolidge. His grounds: commodity price supports would discourage diversified farming and lead to one-crop efforts and possible soil exhaustion.

During the twenties, all this was academic economics. By the early thirties, it had become a matter of downright hunger. With the desperation of the starved, Americans wanted no truck with theory. For every wrong there ought to be a remedy, "there ought to be a law . . . " In this context the Federal Farm Board extended credit to cooperatives and tried, unsuccessfully, to stabilize cotton and wheat prices. Finally in 1933 the Agricultural Adjustment Administration grappled directly with the supply-demand equation by providing for acreage reduction and crop storage. This was the age of the "plowed-under pig and the rotting potato," and tobacco was

"Priming" refers to single-leaf harvesting, which permits each leaf to reach full ripeness. Chemical content varies with leaf's position on the stalk.

Narrow mule-drawn sleds are used to gather tobacco on most farms, since rows are spaced too close for tractors. Need for judgment prevents mechanization.

Tied to sticks, the green leaf is taken to curing barns. These are cube-shaped, twenty or twenty-five feet square. Leaf-hanging is often a family affair.

Leaves are spaced evenly so that each will get its full share of heat. The curing barn is chinked and its roof sealed so that the heat can be regulated.

one of the seven basic commodities to come under AAA. Because most tobacco growers were small farmers, cutbacks were not widely made. But the acreage control put a brake on leaf output, and prices rose somewhat. A second depression in 1938 led to a new farm bill, establishing marketing quotas. These quotas were announced by the Secretary of Agriculture and validated by a two-thirds vote of the farmers concerned. Over-quota sales of tobacco carried a tax equal to 50% of the selling price. Acreage controls and loans against surplus production were continued, and outright "parity payments" to farmers were authorized. In 1942, tobacco price supports were fixed at 90% of parity.

Under the new system, tobacco expansion followed government announcements of increases instead of the market for leaf. The general direction of farm legislation was to curtail farm production to keep prices up. At the same time, manufacturers of cigarettes were attempting—successfully—to broaden the demand for their national brands. As a natural result, during the earlier years of War II, this put tobacco in short supply: not until 1944 did farm output of leaf regain the level of 1939. To keep up with rising cigarette sales, the Company had to dig deeply into its leaf inventory; and to replenish leaf inventory at higher prices, it was necessary to float debenture issues—$100 million in 1942 and a

Firing a barnful of tobacco is a delicate, tiresome process, requiring a vigil of four days or more. If a flue breaks, a whole year's work goes up in smoke.

After curing, Bright leaf is orange or lemon-yellow. Burley and Maryland are air-cured under shade, while Turkish tobacco is cured in sun, covered up at night.

like amount in 1944—plus a $50 million common stock flotation in 1947.

The big squeeze

Flexible parity prices were worked into the 1949 Act, but tobacco supports remained at 90%. With the supply of leaf controlled, the increasing demand for tobacco products after 1940 kept leaf prices on an ever-upward spiral. From the Company's standpoint this worked a double hardship, since retail prices of cigarettes and other packaged products were held rigid by OPA ceilings during War II and again during the Korean War. As a consequence, the profit margin on sales (before corporate income taxes) nar-

rowed from 1940's 13.6% to a low of 6.5% in 1946 and struggled slowly up to 9.3% in 1953. Likewise common stock dividends, which were paid at a $5.00 rate in 1940, shrunk to $3.25 during the war years. After regaining a level of $4.00 during 1949-1953, the indicated rate was increased to $4.40 early in 1954, as the excess profits tax expired.

Financial writers described the Company's situation as a "double squeeze" between fixed cigarette prices on the one hand, propped-up leaf prices and the greater leaf requirements of king-sized cigarettes on the other. Underlying the narrowed margin, however, was the very policy responsible for the Company's growth—the policy of "L.S./M.F.T."

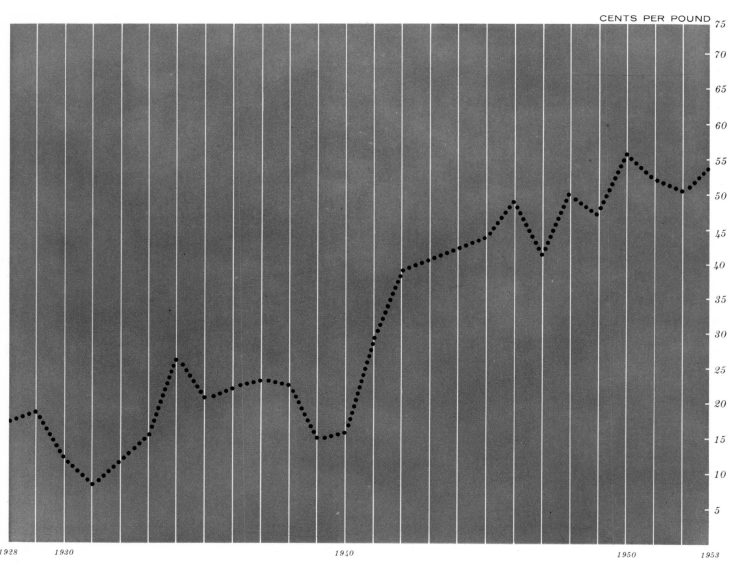

CENTS PER POUND

Because tobacco is still bought in small lots, mass purchasing does not necessarily mean lower leaf cost. Actually, as cigarette business has grown, need for better grades has pushed up prices paid to farmers.

As calculated by Department of Agriculture, farmers' average price for flue-cured leaf, above, has increased 563% since 1931. In every year, American Tobacco's purchase price for Burley and Bright exceeded average.

Under this policy, American Tobacco does not buy to price in the leaf auctions—a fact which seems almost anomalous in the age of cost accounting and expensive distribution. How do the buyers buy? Said one of the Company's Vice Presidents in 1940: "The grade is all important in buying tobacco. The trademark determines the grade. The law of supply and demand—open competition—determines the price. We do not buy to price—if we did we would destroy our trademarks."

In this light, it was not surprising that Riggio should have picked "*Lucky Strike* Means Fine Tobacco" as the most deathless of Hill's carefully-turned phrases. But Riggio, for fifty years a master salesman,

could not ignore the revolution in America's smoking habits. *Lucky Strike* was being hammered down by its own running mates: the Company's twin kings accounted for one of every eight cigarettes sold in 1946, one of every four by 1950, the year of Riggio's succession by Paul Hahn.

As it turned out, the expansion of the king-size market confirmed the importance of leaf and gave the lie to cynics who claimed the public couldn't really distinguish between cigarettes but only between brand names. When the rest of the industry began to create king-size brands, it soon became apparent that the public taste demanded more than added length alone. The "secondary brands" as the

Before War II, an acre of tobacco yielded $185; it now yields $620. This is due not only to the rise in price (chart, opposite page) but to an increase in poundage yield, from 900 to 1,240. Value of the

tobacco crop averages well over $1 billion—about eight percent of the entire U. S. crop value. Some 60% of a typical crop is flue-cured and 28% Burley —the rest Maryland, cigar wrapper and fire-cured.

Paul M. Hahn

trade dubbed them went exactly nowhere. And they were secondary: one appeared without a trace of Turkish leaf, an expensive but necessary "seasoning ingredient" in every successful brand. The upshot, in retrospect, was logical—as recently as 1951, *Pall Mall* and *Tareyton*—rolled from leaf of *Lucky Strike* quality but blended to different formulae—had 90% of the entire king-size market between them. The next year, in a belated bow to the public palate, one of the leading makers kinged its standard cigarette. Others followed. But it was only these "primary blends" which succeeded in the developing king-size market, blends which had already won followings in standard length. As one company after another kinged its principal brand, its standard cigarette began to recede as *Lucky*

Strike had. In war, as the nation's senior general thundered from Tokyo, there is no substitute for victory; and in cigarettes, as Buck Duke discovered in Durham, there is no substitute for fine leaf.

During Vincent Riggio's stewardship, the Big Brand Era had sprung up, flowered and finally faded in favor of the "department store" age of cigarette merchandising. American Tobacco no longer stood or fell on the strength of one advertising slogan: diversification had given American Tobacco a "big three" all its own, the No. 2, No. 4 and No. 7 brands. Riggio, ailing, was ready to vacate the chief executive's chair for the quiet ex-lawyer who had turned brand land upside down. In April, 1950, Paul Hahn became the Company's fifth President.

PARTICULAR PEOPLE

LIKE THE RECIPE for grandmother's mince pie, the blend of a cigarette is as much a tradition as it is a formula. And like any tradition, it lives only as long as there are particular people who will take some pains to preserve it.

These "particular people" are not limited to the 19,000 employees of American Tobacco. Preservation of a great blend like the toasted *Lucky Strike* or the newer *Pall Mall* and *Herbert Tareyton* is rooted in the taste of the consuming public. It is up to the hundreds of Company salesmen—really servicemen—to keep close to that public, to sniff out changes in its taste almost before they occur. There are always new mixtures being tried in Durham, now as in Wash Duke's day the incubating place for new brands. And these experimental blends are constantly being tested at the Richmond research laboratory.

At the other end of the cigarette line, literally at the roots, are scouts from the leaf subsidiary. As the seedlings of the Golden Belt peep up through the soft April loam, these scouts are very close to the farmer himself. They have been working all year with the Agricultural Experiment Stations of the states and the Federal government—watching test crops, trying new fertilizers, collecting leaf samples for analysis. All this leads to advertisements placed by the Company in farm periodicals to show the planter the latest methods to guard his soil and his leaf against tobacco's natural enemies, beetles and fungi. And leaf men are moving spirits behind new advances in tobacco culture, like the experimental growing of Turkish-type leaf in the Carolinas.

Until the early 1940s, manufacturers had kept out of the tobacco patch. Growing leaf had been the farmer's province; processing it, the manufacturer's. Two new influences changed this. First, foreign outlets of tobacco diminished, lowering demand for the grades unsuited for domestic use. At the same time, the growing domestic business needed a larger proportion of the crop. Only a third of the flue-cured crop, for example, was used in domestic cigarettes before War II, compared with two-thirds today.

The second influence was the encroachment of diseases like root rot, black shank and granville wilt. These had been controlled with crop rotation, but Federal acreage restrictions and the resulting one-crop farming gave the pests a chance to "dig in." At this point The American Tobacco Company initiated a program of research in collaboration with Federal and state Experiment Stations. The program's findings are

American Tobacco's research program dates back to 1911; present building in Richmond was erected in 1939. Laboratory now employs a total of 90 people.

Smoking machine, which simulates puffing of human being, was devised by American Tobacco scientists, is now standard apparatus for world's researchers.

disseminated to farmers by the Agricultural Extension Service as well as by the Company's own advertisements.

Typically, the Experiment Stations contract with farmers to grow tobacco from seed of advanced breeding lines, and the Company agrees to buy this leaf at the market average for its grade. The new strains are compared with standard varieties in factory and laboratory tests.

Field experiments began in 1949 in North and South Carolina, Virginia, Kentucky and Tennessee, later being extended to Georgia, Florida and Maryland. The principal emphasis has been on variety improvement, although field survival and increased

yield have also figured. Studies embrace fertilization, topping and suckering practises, sucker control, irrigation, harvesting, curing and other farm operations.

Others followed the Company's lead in this field—Liggett & Myers since 1950, Reynolds since 1951, The Imperial Tobacco Company in 1951 and in 1953, Philip Morris and the Export Leaf Tobacco Company in the last-named year.

The work of the scouts has a practical as well as a long-range value. Before the summer heat has sent up the tall tobacco stalks and ripened the floppy green leaves almost to the size of elephant's ears, specimens of the new crop are inside the tan brick building on the Petersburg Pike. There some sixty-

Leaf scouts go right to the farm for advance line on crop quality. Samples are fully analyzed in the Richmond lab before crops themselves are marketed.

When farmers are readying cured leaf for auction, Company executives are estimating the amounts of suitable cigarette tobacco which will be available.

First step in auction procedure may take place at night. Farmer and warehouseman make up baskets of leaf so that quality is uniform within each one.

Actual sale is confusing ritual of winks, chants, nods and thumb-twitching. Auctioneer and warehouse clerks walk on one side, rival buyers on the other.

odd scientists and trained specialists are breaking down the leaf in their retorts, testing its content of sugar, nicotine, bases. Before a hand of tobacco has appeared on the warehouse floors, the leaf buyers of American Suppliers have an accurate idea of where the best tobacco will be grown, how much of it will be suitable for the Company's blends. If a given crop promises to be unusually poor, the manufacturing Vice Presidents in New York are alerted; often a portion of the Company's needs can be filled from stored leaf in Government warehouses.

At every step of the long journey from seedbed to finished cigarette, the Ph.D.s of the research laboratory are analyzing. They receive leaf from curing barns, from warehouse floors, from hogsheads in the silent storage sheds, from each day's tumbling bins at every factory. After the leaf has been rolled into cigarettes and packages, they are still analyzing samples from the factory, from the distribution pipelines, even from the counters of retail shops.

Like the cigarette tobacco itself, which must age and sweat in the dark before it is ready for blending, an organization must age and sweat its way to maturity. The American Tobacco Company's research lab, the industry's first, was set up in 1911. As its scientists learned of more things to be particular *about*, the laboratory expanded. The present main building was finished in 1939. Today a new wing is

Auctioneer's singsong chant is a means to save his voice, consists of prices repeated over and over. There is no pause between one basket and the next.

Letter "A" on bright cigarette leaf indicates that lot has been "sold American." If farmer feels price is not right, he can turn the ticket and void sale.

Turkish leaf is bought, manipulated and baled by the American Tobacco Company of the Orient. In Turkish ports too shallow for direct loading, barges help.

Orpheus D. Baxalys, a director of American Tobacco, runs the Turkish leaf-buying subsidiary. Baxalys covers entire Middle East, makes his office in Athens.

Another Company director, Hiram R. Hanmer, manages research program. His findings make possible farm ads (opposite page) to improve yield and quality.

being built to double the square footage of working area.

Refinements in processing now accepted as routine are the results of years of painstaking studies, headed since 1932 by Hiram R. Hanmer. Chemical make-up of leaf in its many varieties; effects of processing on aroma; fundamental research on the composition and taste of cigarette smoke—four decades of this lie behind today's manufacturing standards. Recent experiments with farmers themselves, insuring a continuing supply of good quality tobacco, are just another widening of the laboratory's horizon of knowledge.

Controlled construction

One of the things learned by Research Director Hiram Hanmer and his staff is that there is more to cigarette making than leaf, more than the secret flavoring formula sprayed on the sugarless Burley. The strands of shredded tobacco must be long enough to burn evenly, packed tightly enough to avoid loose ends or air pockets—yet they must be packed loosely enough to be free and easy on the draw. The package must be effectively sealed to prevent drying out in transit, the moisture content just right to preserve the full flavor for the smoker. Not only the paper wrap but the very ink on the label must be tested, lest the finished cigarettes absorb alien odors.

The massive routine of inspecting for all this —"statistical quality control"—is the responsibility of Research. Representative samples from each batch of labels, glue, cellophane, cartons, bags, boxes, syrups and extracts must be chemically analyzed and approved before entering the main stream of manufacture and distribution. This is the kind of control which lies behind the rise of the leading brands and the replacement of "roll your own" by the machine-made cigarette. For the taste of a cigarette depends as much on its manufacturing process, physical "construction" and dimensions as on the excellence of its ingredients. This is a fact twenty-seven-year-old Buck Duke sensed when he led the industry into the machine age with his Bonsacks of 1883. It is a fact every cowboy learns when he first rolls his own from *Bull Durham* makin's and the *Riz La Croix* paper attached to the sack. It is a fact which the public has come to appreciate over the years. And it is a fact

TOBACCO field cultivation in the Flue-cured area has an importance not always fully realized by the grower. Actually, cultivation practices have a great influence on the success or failure of the crop. Correct cultivation methods help prevent erosion, help protect the growing plants, and contribute to the development of larger, healthier plants. Federal and State Experiment Stations have conducted tests and studies over a period of years to determine the most efficient and beneficial cultivation methods. The results can be of great value to farmers of the Flue-cured area.

Proper cultivation in the field will help this young tobacco plant develop into a healthy, mature plant of high quality.

Good Field Cultivation Promotes Tobacco Growth

Field of tobacco being cultivated with harrow and mule (the old method, but still being used by many).

There are many definite benefits to be gained by paying close attention to proper field cultivation. Chief among these benefits is the control of weeds and grasses. Weeds and grasses rob the crop of water and plant nutrients which it otherwise would get. In this manner proper cultivation may aid in the conservation of soil moisture and plant nutrients. Also, weedy and grassy fields are usually more heavily infested with insects. The weeds and grass provide protective cover and breeding spots for them.

HELPS PREVENT EROSION

A sound cultivation program has its beginning before the crop is planted. The soil should first be well-prepared by plowing and disking. The row layout should be such as to afford good drainage with a minimum of erosion. If the rows have too much fall, erosion and excessive loss of water may occur. On the other hand, if the rows do not drain, the plants may drown during wet periods, or water may break the rows, causing a wash through the field.

Flue-cured tobacco is planted on a ridge in which most, if not all, of the fertilizer has been placed. On land that is well-drained, a moderate ridge itself has very little effect upon the growth of the plant. Three or four cultivations should have taken place before the arrival (in normal years) of heavy summer rains, so that the channels between the ridges can provide places deep enough for the water to run, preventing sheet erosion, and stopping water from accumulating in a few low places, causing gullies. On flat, imperfectly drained land, ridging provides channels for draining the field during rainy periods and may therefore influence plant growth. Ridging decreases the chances of the soil becoming water-logged.

Flue-cured tobacco, predominantly, is planted on the light-textured soils (sands and

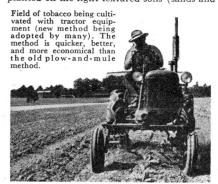

Field of tobacco being cultivated with tractor equipment (new method being adopted by many). The method is quicker, better, and more economical than the old plow-and-mule method.

sandy loams). On soils of this nature, the beneficial effect of cultivation is that of controlling weeds and grasses. On the heavy-textured soils, the principal effect also seems to be that of controlling weeds and grasses, but, in addition, cultivation aids in the infiltration of water. Shallow cultivation accomplishes the purpose in both cases and need only be performed often enough to control the weeds and grasses.

AVOID INJURY TO ROOTS

The plant nutrients and water which the plant must get for proper growth are absorbed by the roots of the plant from the soil. Anything that interferes with root development will therefore affect the uptake of water and nutrients by the plant and, in turn, influence the growth of the plant.

Cultivation should therefore be performed in such a manner as to cause the minimum damage to the root system. Shallow cultivation performed often enough to control grass and weeds has invariably given better results than deep cultivation. Excessive cultivation will tend to dry out the soil.

The rotary hoe does a good job of cultivation when the plants are small. For the later cultivation there are several types of horse-drawn and tractor equipment that will do a good job.

For more specific information on row layout and cultivation, contact your County Agent, other Extension Workers, or Vocational Agriculture Teachers.

The American Tobacco Company
INCORPORATED
Copyright 1953

THE AMERICAN TOBACCO COMPANY WORKS WITH EXPERIMENT STATIONS TO PRODUCE FINER TOBACCO

now expressed in the Company's advertising copy, "made better to taste better."

The first "particular people" in the chain of cigarette blending are, of course, the farmers themselves. Starting with a spoonful of tiny seed—enough to plant several acres—the American tobacco farmer nurses his plants just as does his Cuban counterpart in Pinar del Rio. His seedbed is hoed, "burned over" and raked before the seeds are planted, and covered with cheesecloth to shelter the new sprouts from the raw weather of spring. After the frost season is past, the little tobacco plants are set in rows, like corn, about three or four feet apart.

Although the summer sun makes their growth rapid, the straight tobacco stalks cannot be left on their own. When the flower buds first appear at their tips, the plants are "topped" so that all the vital nourishment goes into the leaves. The sidewise sprouts or "suckers" must also be removed, for the same reason.

All during the growing season, the farmer watches the sky and ponders the weathermap. Hail can destroy a field of tobacco completely; heavy rainfall can make the leaves too thin, too washed-out; and excessive drought can do the reverse. Meanwhile, the hoeing and weeding and spraying must go on continually.

When the leaves are ripe they are stripped individually from the stalks, a process known as "priming." Twined to tobacco sticks, they are hung in the curing barn to dry. In some parts of the world, this is not a complicated phase—Burley and Maryland leaf is air-cured, simply hung at normal temperature until the tobacco is dry. Turkish tobacco is spread in the sun. But Bright tobacco, which has constituted half or more of every big blend ever since W. Duke of Durham began to roll cigarettes, is a different matter. The flue-curing needed to drive out all the moisture while retaining the prized lemon or orange color is a touchy and exhausting business.

Thomas Hart Benton was among artists commissioned to paint tobacco scenes like this, "Outside the Curing Barn."

"Tobacco Talk" was painted by James Chapin, conveys the serious attitude of farmer, buyer and warehouseman.

When the barn is filled with hanging tobacco leaves, it is not enough simply to light the fires in the "kilns" outside and let the heat rush through the flues to do the rest. The inside temperature must be kept within twenty degrees of the outside reading anywhere from one and a half to two days. During all of this time the farmer must be at the barn, using his thermometer and, if necessary, the ventilators.

As the curing begins to bring out the yellow color, the heat is increased. For sixteen or eighteen hours more, the vigil continues until the tobacco is dry enough to curl. But the end is not yet. Unless the stems and veins are just as dry as the leaf, the sap will backflow and scald it. Accordingly, another sixteen hours of high temperature follows. Before the stems are "killed," the farmer will have put in three or four days and nights without sleep. And even after the curing is finished, the fires must be banked gradually: inside the barn, the flues are red-hot and still dangerous.

After this ordeal, grading seems child's play. There will be some good tobacco in a crop and some that is not so good. So the farmer and his family will sort out the best quality leaf from the average run, tying each grade into bunches or "hands" of a dozen or two dozen leaves. Five months after the powdery seed was put to bed under the cheesecloth, the tobacco is ready to go to market.

The next "particular people" to figure in the cigarette cycle are the leaf buyers who work under American Suppliers President James F. Strickland. They are in the market towns of Georgia and Northern Florida when the southernmost Bright crop "breaks" early in the summer. They move north to the Carolinas and Virginia as the more northerly flue-cured leaf comes to market, then west to the Burley markets of Kentucky and Tennessee which do not close until February of the following year. Strickland makes his headquarters in Durham, while his Executive Vice President, John Dowd, has his office in Louisville. Dowd, who not only smokes cigarettes and cigars but chews a twist of "the strongest, blackest One Sucker I can find," specializes in the Burley markets. Although Bright and Burley make up the bulk of most blends, a "seasoning" proportion of Turkish leaf is needed. The American Tobacco Company of the Orient, under the resident managership of Orpheus D. Baxalys, buys, manipulates* and bales the Turkish leaf where it is grown. Baxalys operates out of Athens, Greece. A fourth variety of tobacco, Maryland, appears on its own markets in and around Baltimore; Maryland is a large brown leaf, much like Burley in appearance. It is unusually free-burning and contributes a characteristic nutlike flavor.

Sold American

For the farmer, a loose-leaf auction in a market town is something of a festival. It is the payoff following a whole year's work and worry; the price

---

*As used in the trade, the word refers to unstringing, sorting and cleaning the tobacco.

his leaf brings is the measure of his skill, and the trip to town is a kind of social event analogous to the barn-buildings of colonial times.

Between them, farmer and warehouseman grade the tobacco and lay it out in long rows of baskets on the selling floor. Much of this is done at night, so that sales can begin early in the morning. When they do, the buyer will be very much on the spot. Alongside him will be rivals from other large cigarette companies, from the British manufacturers, from the leaf brokers who supply smaller manufacturers with their tobacco. This group—perhaps eight or ten bidders—will form a line on one side of the rows of baskets. On the other side facing them are the warehouseman, his auctioneer, and two or three record-keepers. Without breaking step, the two files will move slowly down the line from basket to basket, farmers and their families craning their necks to see, the warehouse hustlers waiting with their dollies to

Durham leaf sheds built around 1900 were all brick, some with fancy turrets. Company no longer stores in

brick. Louvered sheds of corrugated metal became standard after 1911. Current storages resemble one below.

Stemming is a little-known but crucial stage in the manufacture of cigarettes. The late Douglas Brashear, a director of American Tobacco, oversaw stemmeries.

Rigid hogsheads—giant 1,000-pound barrels—were outmoded after War II. "Bull gangs" once handled the heavy casks, painfully dismantled them to get at leaf.

move the leaf off the floor after the bidding is over.

Contrary to popular impression, the chant of the auctioneer is not the hardest part of the transactions to understand. He uses a singsong delivery to save his voice, merely repeating the price over and over as the bidding takes place—"sixty-eight-sixty-eight-sixty-eight-eight-eight, sixty-nine-nine-nine, seventy-seventy-seventy-seventy-one-seventy-one — sold American!" More difficult to pick out are the buying and bidding signals themselves. Most buyers make their bids as unobtrusively as possible, using a wink, a barely perceptible nod, a twist of the thumb. Their eyes flick between the auctioneer and the piles of tobacco: in a glance they must distinguish between the smooth, silky "cutting leaf" that is suitable for first-quality cigarette blends and leaf of almost identical color which is not. Once in a while, a buyer will confirm his visual judgment by fingering a handful of tobacco.

When the auctioneer's brief handclap closes a sale, the initials of the buyer's company—"A" for American—are crayoned on the ticket. Should the farmer feel the price is too low, he can "turn his ticket," void the sale, and try his luck the next day or even on another market. Or he can sell the leaf to the government at support prices.

Bringing in the leaves

When leaf is trucked from the warehouses it is in "farmer's order"—some too wet, some too dry. As soon as it can be unpacked it is strung on racks, hand by hand, and put through "reordering" or "redrying" machines. These first take all the moisture out of the tobacco, then re-moisten it to the extent needed for aging. When the treated tobacco comes out of the long redriers, it is prized into hogsheads and trundled off to its long sleep in the aging sheds.

American Tobacco now has 249 of these huge sheds in seven great clusters, each close to a manufacturing center. They contain about $600 million worth of leaf. More than 200 of them are divided among the four "cigarette towns"—Durham, Richmond, Louisville and Reidsville, each employing roughly 3,000 people.* Some tobacco is stemmed while it is still "green" or fresh from the markets,

---

*Lucky Strike and Pall Mall are made at all four centers. Durham is the center for Herbert Tareyton and for the small-volume brands carried over from the past—Sweet Caporal, Johnny Walker, Mecca, "111," Lord Salisbury, Sovereign and the Turkish Pall Malls, Melachrino, Natural, Egyptian Prettiest and Straights. Richmond is the center for smoking tobacco brands, although Bull Durham is still made in its namesake city.

Power-driven "leaf lifts" now receive shipped leaf, packed in a hogshead of modern design. Its wired plywood staves make a single, flexible side wrap.

Tops and bottoms are uniformly sized, also plywood, can be quickly removed without damage after metal bands around the hogshead's sides have been snipped.

and put to age in strip form; the greater part is stemmed after "sweating it out" in the corrugated-steel storage buildings.

Cigarette tobacco can be readied for blending in two ways: by stemming, which denotes removal of the midrib leaf by leaf, or by thrashing batches of leaf into bits, the heavier stem fragments being separated from the whirling mix by gravity. Unlike some manufacturers, American Tobacco has never thrashed its cigarette leaf. This method is cheaper, but it breaks up the tobacco excessively or leaves bits of woody stem in the mixture—a danger not present when the midrib is removed whole. In 1946 the Company developed a new type of stemming machine and

granted the selling rights to American Machine & Foundry. This is the machine presently used by those leaf dealers and manufacturers who stem rather than flail.

Stemming—always preceded by a re-readying process of vacuum sweating—is the last step performed by American Suppliers. At this point the strip leaf enters the factories of the parent Company itself.

The merry-go-round

Here begins a long and complicated fusing of the different types of tobacco into the blend. The Burley leaf is dipped separately with the flavoring mixture from the factory's "kitchen"; in the case of

Aside from ease of removal, the new hogsheads are seldom damaged in the receiving room, can be used again without making a trip to the carpenter shop.

All incoming leaf is spread out on a moving belt, where any foreign matter is removed. Newly-bought tobacco in "farmer's order" requires reconditioning.

After inspection, new tobacco is fed into redrying machines. These remove all moisture from the leaf, then remoisten it to proper degree prior to aging.

After redrying, some tobacco is trucked unstemmed to the storage sheds, where it undergoes a chemical change and periodic "sweats" for two or more years.

Lucky Strike cigarettes, it is toasted—a four-step operation involving drying, the application of superheated steam, cooling, and remoistening with saturated steam. Then the four kinds of leaf are tumbled together and piled in huge cubes in the "bulking room." There it remains for a night and a day while a subtle intermingling of the various oils and aromas takes place. Like the mysterious process of "sweating" in storage, the change effected by bulking has not been reduced to exact chemical terms. It does, however, improve the final blend, although not all tobacco manufacturers bulk.

Following this brief nap, the mixture goes to the cutting machines where the strip is shredded into

the tiny strands that make up a cigarette. The *Lucky Strike* mixture passes under a battery of ultra-violet lamps. The tobacco is now parceled into "saratogas" or trunk-like boxes—green for *Lucky Strike* and red for *Pall Mall*. After standing overnight in the saratogas, the final blend will have been remixed some sixty times for the sake of complete uniformity. (For the same reason the flavoring essence is mixed in Richmond, then divided among the four making centers.) The last "change of trains" takes place in a little ring of wheeled trolleys called a "merry-go-round." From here the golden, shredded mix is carted to the making machines.

Remarkable as the cigarette machine is—it

Stems are removed prior to manufacture. When this is done before aging, tobacco is said to be "green stemmed." Stems can be pulled (above) or "thrashed."

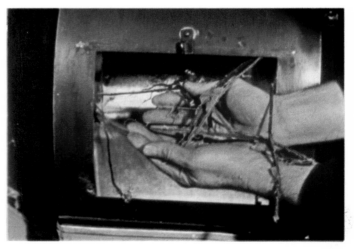

Although thrashing is cheaper, all Company leaf is stemmed individually. This insures that the entire midrib is removed and the cigarette free of woody bits.

prints the brand name, rolls the paper ribbon around a steady stream of tobacco, seals the continuous tube with milk paste, and shears off twenty cigarettes per second—human watchfulness is needed. The operator must see that the hopper is full, that the flow of paste, paper and tobacco is synchronized, that the circumference of the emerging tube is perfect, that the speed is not too great for precision results. The catcher gives the finished cigarettes a last look as she piles them in her tray; she is a pitcher as well, for the imperfect ones must be picked out and pitched into the waste box. As a further check, batches of cigarettes are weighed either by hand or electronically, to control the final weight within narrow tolerances. Automatic packers, so sensitive that they can detect and throw out a pack containing one defective cigarette, quickly seal the fresh rolls in foil, paper, tax stamp, cellophane and tear tape.

During all this, operators have been testing the feel of the tobacco, checking temperature, adjusting valves to control the moisture. Each floor has its testing desks, where boxes of tobacco are tested under the electronic moisture meter developed by American Tobacco. The factory itself is a giant air-conditioned humidor—in a typical plant the stairwells and auxiliary rooms are outside the main wall shell, so that no non-tobacco odors or street dust can intrude on the mixing process.

To get and keep the best people to carry out this complex production routine, personnel administration is handled at the top management level—Vice Presidents Fowler and Crowe for manufacturing people, Vice President Coon for the main office force. Each regular employee is covered by life insurance at no cost to him, the principal amounting to about twice his yearly salary, with a maximum of $20,000. Medical insurance for in-hospital doctors' fees is also provided by the Company. In 1949 a retirement pension plan was put into effect, and this too involves no contribution by the employee. To this "loyalty down" American Tobacco's people respond with "loyalty up": almost half of the cigarette, smoking tobacco and leaf department employees have service records of 10 years, and nearly one in ten are quarter-century veterans.

Legally, American Tobacco was born in 1890 or in 1904, whichever date of incorporation is chosen. But the present Company really dates from the last months of 1911. Before that time the organization was tied together largely by purse strings. Its various branches and subsidiaries were still separate companies in every sense but the financial. Each had its own brands, its own manager, its own traditions, its own standards of quality. Only after these parts had been integrated did American Tobacco become an organic whole as well as a legal entity.

Manufacture is supervised by two Vice Presidents, Preston L. Fowler (left) and John A. Crowe (center), *assisted by William H. Ogsbury. Fowler and Crowe each have over forty years manufacturing experience.*

124

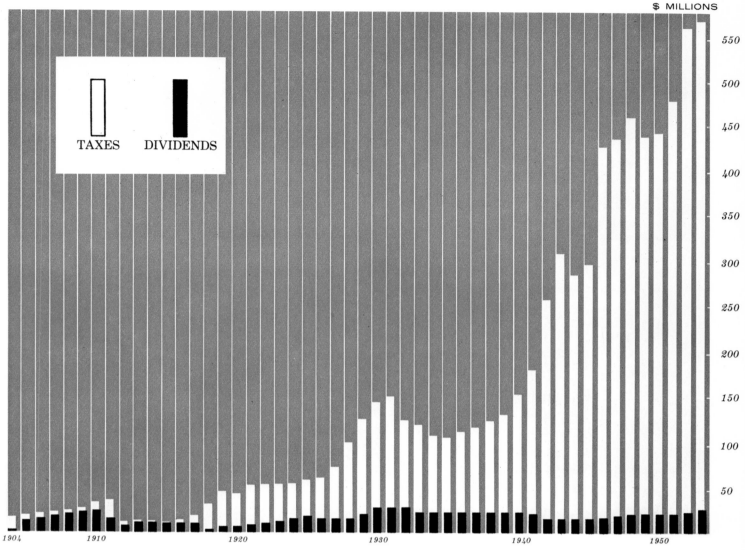

$ MILLIONS

550

500

450

400

350

300

250

200

150

100

50

TAXES   DIVIDENDS

1904   1910   1920   1930   1940   1950

In 1953 Company sales were $1,088 billion, of which $570 million was paid to the U. S. Government for revenue stamps, income taxes, excess profits taxes and capital stock taxes. City and state levies on American's products, income and property brought *the total tax bill to $630 million. Cash dividends to stockholders (black bars) have not exceeded $30 million since 1932, though taxes show a steep rise. About 90% of Federal tax payments (white bars) are for cigarette excise stamps, now costing 8c per pack.*

To make a whole greater than the sum of its parts, to develop *esprit*, to make quality control a matter of honor as well as regulation—all this took time. Perhaps the greatest single spur to it was the *Lucky Strike* cigarette. As its volume grew too great for a single factory to handle, the new product brought widely-scattered people together in a common effort. A manufacturing tradition grew up around the master blenders and leaf men, the Penns, the Lipscombs, the Neileys, the Stricklands, the Fowlers and the Crowes. "Upstage"—*i.e.*, in the headquarters offices—differences are apparent between one regime and the next. Down South in the

plants they are not. It is easy to overlook the fact that George Washington Hill only promoted the word "toasting," but did not invent the process.

Candor requires the observation that manufacturing people have always been a little dubious about promotion and exploitation because it put them on the spot, and put competitors on notice at the same time. The manufacturing men felt consumers could see and taste the difference without being hit over the head with a slogan. They sought quality for its own sake, not for the sake of making claims. Rightly or wrongly, they felt the product could sell itself.

As it enters the toasting machine, leaf is in strip form. It travels on a moving belt through heating chambers, is then remoistened with saturated steam.

The blend of Burley, Bright, Maryland and Turkish tobaccos stands in great cubes for 24 hours. This "bulking" permits essential oils to intermingle.

In any event, the permanent cadre of American Tobacco, the stabilizing core of the operation, is still the Department of Manufacture (which includes the Leaf Department). Advertising agencies can change; new Presidents may bring new policies for sales, for finance, for public relations. But it would be unthinkable and, indeed, impossible to replace the leaf buyers and the seasoned factorymen. They make the product, and the product makes the Company.

Penalties and payout

Looking at all this from the shady canyons of Wall Street, the security analysts of a cost-cutting age sometimes register puzzlement. Why, they ask

Treasurer Harry Hilyard, is American's workforce almost 60% larger than any other in the industry although its unit cigarette production is only 24% or 25% greater than the next largest company? The answer is threefold: first, plant diversification among four major centers quadruples some of the overhead; second, the Company is more fully integrated than most of its rivals, all the way down to its own production of tobacco sacks (by Golden Belt Manufacturing Company, a subsidiary) and the growing of its own domestic cigar wrapper (by Hatheway-Steane Corporation, another subsidiary). And third, the factory routine is kept more elaborate: in addition to the "catcher," who watches the output of each cigarette

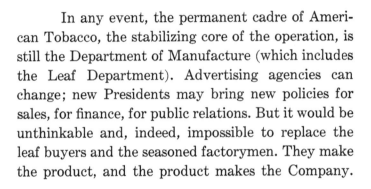

From the bulking rooms tobacco goes to shredding machines. Long, slender strands are necessary for smooth smoking, so laboratory samples are taken.

Flavored, blended and shredded, the mixture now goes into "saratogas" for another intermingling period. Electronic meters register leaf's moisture content.

"Merry-go-round" trolleys each take a small portion of saratoga's contents. After this final remixing, the blend is wheeled away to the making machines.

Machines turn out "endless" cigarette which is cut to length after paper ribbon is folded, filled and printed with brand mark. Catcher loads cigarettes.

maker, each machine has its own operator. Some manufacturers employ only one operator for every two machines. When a young researcher from the Richmond lab told Vice President Crowe he had found a way to save $100,000 a year in manufacturing, he got a level stare and this answer: "Young man, you stick to quality and let us worry about the money."

As recently as 1951, a financial editor described this attitude as a "fetish of quality." At first, recalls Hilyard, the Board of Directors resented the remark. Later, however, they realized it was a compliment and even used it in TV commercials for *Lucky Strike.*

In manufacturing, to be sure, the Company incurs what business journalists call the "penalty of leadership." It was the first to make and package cigarettes on the same floor (in Brooklyn) the better to preserve freshness in the cigarettes. After years of trial and error (and expense), the Richmond lab turned out the automatic smoking machine now used by researchers in the rest of the industry. In the long run the quality fetish pays out.

One place where it pays out is in advertising expense. Madison Avenue's admen are likely to think in terms of total dollar expenditures. Since War II, however, the Company's dollar costs in this area have not been the industry's greatest, although its unit

While catcher picks imperfect tubes from her tray, inspectress with scales weighs a counted number of finished cigarettes. Little variation is permitted.

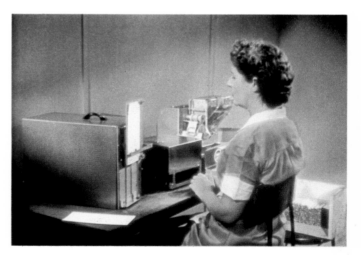

Electric weigh station checks single cigarettes as well as counted groups. Packing must be loose for smooth drawing, tight enough to avoid air pockets.

Samples from all production centers go to Richmond laboratory for quality control tests. Cigarettes are tumbled in cylinder to check on "loose ends."

Every lot of cigarette paper is sampled before it enters production stream. This machine spots flaws and another measures strength or "breaking point."

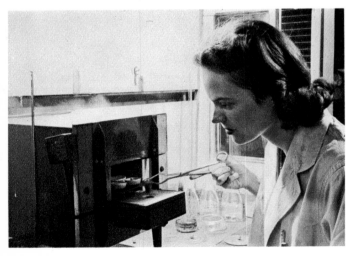

To doublecheck factory moisture meters, tobacco is weighed, heated dry in this oven and weighed again. Difference is accurate measure of moisture content.

volume and dollar receipts have been. In other words, the Company spends far less to advertise each thousand cigarettes than any of its four rivals—actually, the unit ad cost has been only slightly more than *half* the industry average over the last fifteen years. Shareholders who raise the question of advertising millions are surprised to learn that they reduce to about one-third of a cent per pack (the Federal excise tax alone being 8c as this is written).

The Hahn school

The particular man who best symbolizes the Company's particular people is President Paul Hahn, who also reflects the changed temper of the times. Unlike Hill, who followed the pattern of one-man rule established by the early captains of industry, Hahn is of the committee school of management. His is a rule of reason, of consultation, of calculated rather than spur-of-the-moment decision. Remarkably enough, the Hahn brand of management strengthened even while George Hill was alive, for Hahn was the brain behind the rise of *Pall Mall*, now challenging *Lucky Strike* and *Camel* for the No. 1 spot among all brands. Hahn, perhaps, has typified the Company's basic management longer than his tenure as President (since early 1950) might suggest: he conducted stockholder meetings not only for Hill but for Vincent Riggio. Without any fanfare, Hahn has come to be the leader of the tobacco industry as well. In 1951 he broke a long manufacturers' silence— dating from the 1941 Battle of Lexington—to tell the National Association of Tobacco Distributors that "it's not enough to *be* right—you've also got to *look* right." And late in 1953, when a few scientists were publicizing skin cancer in mice as having some bearing on lung cancer in humans, Hahn was first to speak out in defense of smoking. "With all respect to the sincerity of those who have been working in the field . . . there has been much loose talk on the subject . . . no one has yet proved that lung cancer in any human being is directly traceable to tobacco or to its product in any form . . . " His stand led the press to treat the sensational announcements as the allegations they were; scientists whose experiments had given cigarette smoke a clean bill of health began to see their findings publicized also. The upshot of the science scare was organization of the Tobacco Industry Re-

See why LUCKIES TASTE BETTER!

LUCKY STRIKE "IT'S TOASTED"

CIGARETTES

L.S./M.F.T.

© A.T. Co.

PRODUCT OF

The American Tobacco Company

AMERICA'S LEADING MANUFACTURER OF CIGARETTES

How to prove to yourself Luckies are made better—to taste cleaner, fresher, smoother

Strip the paper from a Lucky by carefully tearing down the seam from end to end. Be sure it's from a newly opened pack, and that you don't dig into the tobacco. Then gently lift out the tobacco.

Free from loose ends

Here's why Luckies taste cleaner: You can see that Luckies hold together without crumbling—without loose ends to get in your mouth and spoil the taste. Lucky Strike remains a perfect cylinder of clean tobacco—round, firm and fully packed.

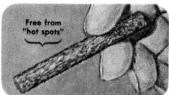

Free from "hot spots"

Here's why Luckies taste fresher: Note how free Luckies are from air spaces—those "hot spots" that give you a harsh, stale taste. Luckies' long strands of fresh, good-tasting tobacco give you a fresh, smooth smoke.

Here's why Luckies taste smoother: L.S./M.F.T., Lucky Strike means fine tobacco—fine, light, naturally mild tobacco. So, for a smoke that's *cleaner, fresher, smoother,* for tobacco that's truly mild, for a cigarette that tastes better ... make your next carton Lucky Strike!

FOR A CLEANER, FRESHER, SMOOTHER SMOKE...
Be Happy-GO LUCKY!

Translation of laboratory facts into interesting copy is a major advertising problem. Each element in this 1953 layout traces to a specific stage in the quality control routine—the tumble test for loose ends; strand length control to avoid any air pockets; pre-market analysis to insure purchase of light, mild leaf. Strip test to prove "round, firm and fully packed" claim is latter-day outgrowth of George Hill's "selling principle of demonstration," is used by salesmen as an aid in direct sampling.

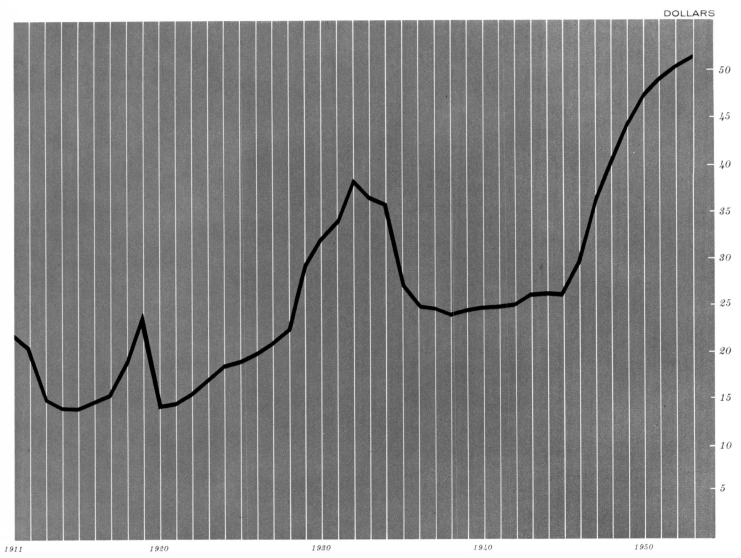

DOLLARS

1911　　　　　　1920　　　　　　1930　　　　　　1940　　　　　　1950

Financial progress, from the point of view of the common stockholder, is traced by chart of tangible book value per common share. (Asset valuations of trademarks and goodwill are deducted throughout.) Sudden dip in 1920 came with issuance of new class of B Common, diluting equity; 1935 dip was result of commuting brand lease of Tobacco Products Corp., a move involving outright purchase of Melachrino and Herbert Tareyton brands, thereby reducing cash. Assets are mainly stored leaf, plant and capital.

search Committee, the industry's first associative effort. Significantly, it was Hahn who chairmanned the first few months' meetings, beginning in December of 1953. Significant, too, was the fact that Hahn's own move was no last-ditch public-relations gambit: in previous years, the Company had contributed heavily to basic research through the Medical College of Virginia, the Damon Runyon Fund, the University of Chicago, and other leading institutions.

Under Hahn, too, the Company's stockholder relations took on a new look. During Hill's brusque regime, complaints about "too much incentive compensation" for executives were frequent. But in 1950

and again in 1951, voluntary cuts in the top-level rates were made: Hahn himself receives less pay as President than he did as Vice President.

Except for the leaf and manufacturing men, Hahn's executives are almost interchangeable. Vice President Harvey, who as chief of sales is completing the regeneration of the field forces, was moved to his present post from Treasurer. Treasurer Harry Hilyard once was sales manager for the west-of-Detroit area. Purchasing Vice President Richard J. Boylan has worked in the legal department and as Secretary. Director Alfred Bowden, who once worked for Charlie Penn, has been assistant to three Presidents—

Hill, Riggio and Hahn. And James Coon, Vice President and Comptroller, has come up through several departments. As custodian of the Company's accounting and financial records, Coon has carried the guiding principle of diversification even into his department: a ghost office is maintained in Trenton against the possibility of any interruption in New York operations. All operations except for final cost accounting can be transferred to New Jersey in a single day, so that collections and disbursements need not stop in an emergency.

The older men are partly teachers, partly decision-makers. In addition to building a corps of young salesmen to nurture the Company's growing volume, E. A. Harvey is training young sales executives to handle them. The same is true of other seasoned executives. William Ogsbury, a veteran of the old Tobacco Products organization, is considered to be one of the country's best cigarette men. His work as assistant chief of manufacture takes him and his know-how to all four cigarette centers. John Hutchings, an American Suppliers Vice President and one of the oldest leaf men in point of service, can take a raw recruit who doesn't know a B Grade from a bull's foot and make a good buyer out of him. In this respect, the senior executives' nicknames are revealing—in his day Lipscomb was called "Uncle Jim," and Preston Fowler, Vice President in charge of

manufacture, is now referred to as "Daddy Fowler." Their postwar efforts to develop young executives have made the management two or three deep at every position, perhaps for the first time in the Company's history.

Under Coon's comptrollership, with A. Leroy Janson as Auditor, the Company's accounting and capital structure have been modernized. (Even the by-laws were rewritten under him: the originals, for instance, made no provision for rescheduling a directors' meeting which falls on a holiday. And they provided a penalty of $20 for any "violation of ethics" by a director!) In recent years, the most obvious change has been elimination of non-voting B common stock. Such issues were "common" during the great business expansion before War I, but are undemocratic in the age of the small stockholder. The practise of charging interest on stored tobacco leaf to the cost of production was also discontinued. This practise had the effect of inflating the dollar value of the finished goods inventory—by $1.2 million the year before it was eliminated.

The most dramatic change, however, revolved around the controversial item of "brand goodwill." Most of the subsidiaries acquired by Duke were bought for their brands, which were carried at $101,324,964.07 in the last year of the combination. After the trust's dissolution, other items were added:

Financial officers include Vice President James R. Coon (left), under whom Company accounting practice *was modernized; A. LeRoy Janson, Auditor; and Harry L. Hilyard, Treasurer. Each man is also a director.*

Herbert Tareyton cigarettes are cork-tipped by an attachment to the standard making machine. Unlike many rivals, Tareyton has always used genuine cork.

Hopper of packaging machine permits last onceover before packs are sealed. Machine itself, however, throws out packs containing imperfect cigarettes.

at the end of 1913, the *Lucky Strike* and *Tuxedo* brands, along with sixteen others acquired from the Patterson Company, were carried at $594,025.38; the Butler brands, including *Pall Mall, Omar, Lord Salisbury, Sovereign, Egyptienne Straights* and thirty-four others, were book-valued at $364,249.67.

In 1918 the U. S. Government, for the purpose of determining excess profits tax liability, computed the Company's goodwill at $138,826,000. By 1947 the total appeared on the balance sheet as $54,099,-430.40, although the market price of common stock outstanding reflected a $187 million valuation of the intangibles. The $54 million items, which dated back to the brand-buying days before 1911, did not include

the twenty-year investment in building the fame of *Lucky Strike*. This was not capitalized but charged to current expenses year by year. Since the $54 million was unrealistic, and since computation of a new figure would be difficult if not impossible, the only solution was to list the value of "brands, trademarks, patents, goodwill, etc." at $1. Hill would never hear of any such "writing down," and it was not until June 1950, just after Paul Hahn became president, that the write-off was effected.

Inside board

Any decision made in the corporation's name, whether it concerns the marketing of a new cigarette

Each score of smokes is sealed with a layer of foil laminated to paper, a printed label, and a sheath of moisture-proof cellophane. Stamp helps seal top.

Insertion of packages ten to a carton also permits visual inspection. Five cartons containing 1,000 cigarettes comprise the sales unit within the trade.

Electronic searcher closes perfect cartons, stops automatically if carton contains less than ten full packages or if aluminum foil is missing from any.

Packing machine counts fifty cartons, pushes them into a cardboard case. Operator's only function is to feed a steady supply of cases into his machine.

or, sometimes, the reply to a stockholder's question, is likely to represent the considered judgment of the management group rather than an individual executive's bright idea. One reason is that American Tobacco has an "inside board"—all its directors are men actually engaged in the Company's business. In effect, these directors meet every day, since they normally dine together in an uptown room reserved for them. Like Hahn, they abhor decisions based on mere expediency. During the "double squeeze" of the Korean War years, when the rising cost of leaf could not be recovered in retail prices, the obvious temptation was to cut the dividend to provide working cash and keep the bank loans down. But Hilyard recalls

the board was reluctant to cut the cash payments even if stock dividends were substituted: such a move, said the Treasurer, "would be cramming financing down the throats" of the more than 80,000 stockholders. Their stand had its reward on March 5, 1952, when $100 million—half in common stock, half in debentures—was raised on the securities markets. Fully 97% of the new common was bought by the offering time, and the remainder snapped up on the exchange in a few minutes.

Despite the squeeze, the Company's leaf mortgage has been whittled steadily. In 1944, with product prices frozen solid and leaf up 130% from prewar levels, debt (both funded and short-term)

Before cases are sealed, a machine weighs each one and records it. Flashing red light indicates a case of non-standard weight, which is removed from line.

Sealed cases, each containing 10,000 cigarettes, go literally to the ends of the earth. Cigarettes are probably the world's most widely distributed goods.

133

Sleeping tobacco, in storage sheds like these near Reidsville, North Carolina, are American Tobacco's most valuable assets in more ways than one. Dollar *value of Company's leaf inventory as of December 31, 1953 was about $600 million. To hold it all, there were 249 storage buildings near the factory cities.*

amounted to 72.4% of inventory. In ten years it has been whittled to 49.9% of inventory, against the upward trend shown by the rest of the industry.

Particular President

The election of Paul Hahn marked off a new era for the Company if not, indeed, for the industry as a whole. Unlike his predecessors Hahn had not begun as a salesman; he was one of a new breed, the whole man of management, qualified to tie the work of many specialists into a single corporate effort. Unlike Buck Duke, he had more than sales volume to worry about; unlike George Hill, he could not concentrate almost wholly on the advertising program. Like the chief executives of other billion-dollar corporations (a category the Company reached in 1952), Hahn performs a balancing act, mediating the interests of the public, the employees, the stockholders. The corporation of Duke's day had been a private enterprise in the narrow sense of that term; today's

corporation is a public institution in every one of its aspects—except, naturally, for the "trade secrets" of blending and selling techniques.

Hahn's first year-end letter, appearing in the annual report for 1950, announced new policies in sales and advertising. The sales force was to be expanded further. The "Be Happy—Go *Lucky*" theme, used previously by the Company, was again introduced into the advertising. To oversee the sales recruitment Edmund Harvey, the veteran trouble shooter, was moved from Treasurer to Vice President for sales.

The new pipeline to the public was not simply a new slogan or a new pitch, although that was part of it. It involved a reshuffling of media so as to really cover the national waterfront. Hill had emphasized radio as superseding print media—which it did, to some extent. But it was his custom to run his print campaigns "in every English-language daily" (except for trade papers and the like). At one point there were over 1,700 of these on the *Lucky Strike* list. This across-the-board method, however, gave relatively light coverage of rural and semi-rural population, which is still reflected in the Company's rural sales of certain products. During the Second World War, Hill pulled out of papers and magazines almost completely, refusing to compete with war news for public attention.

After V-J Day, television loomed as the giant medium of the future. Here *Lucky Strike* vied with its own running mate; the Company's first full-fledged television program* was "The Big Story," a sales vehicle for *Pall Mall* cigarettes inaugurated in 1949. In 1950 a permanent *Lucky Strike* TV show got under way with "Your *Lucky Strike* Theatre," produced by Robert Montgomery. (In 1954 this hour was renamed "The American Tobacco Theatre.")

In the second year of Hahn's presidency, the overall ad program was "rationalized." The profusion of "spots" for *Lucky Strike* commercials was dropped; in their place the advertising department sought to emphasize programs appealing to every taste—the Montgomery show for those partial to serious drama, the televised Hit Parade for everybody, Clifton Fadiman's "This is Show Business" for light listening. Later the Fadiman show was replaced by Ann Sothern in "Private Secretary," a situation comedy, and by Jack Benny, the perennial thirty-nine-year-old who is, perhaps, broadcasting's most entrenched comedian. As TV stations sprang up and the FTC's "freeze" on ultra-high-frequency licenses was thawed in 1953, these programs approached saturation coverage: by the end of 1954, video stations were expected to cover more than 90% of the national market.

On the print side of the program (now accounting for about a quarter of the ad budget), the former long list of publications gave way to a more selective schedule designed, like the TV effort, to leave no gaps in coverage. Farm papers were used to reach the grassroots; the women's market, reached by the new food store magazines, got a bigger play than before. The great mass circulation weeklies, rather than the

---

*Technically, *Lucky Strike* got in the first TV lick with sponsorship of big-time college football telecasts in 1947, followed by "Barney Blake, Police Reporter" in 1948. But Barney was never fully fledged, being taken off the air after only thirteen weeks.

As network television spread, advertising budgets changed drastically. Most funds now go into video. Pall Mall's "Big Story" is a carryover from radio.

Reaching all kinds of people requires several kinds of program. The American Tobacco Theatre, produced by Robert Montgomery, strikes serious dramatic note.

Jack Benny (left), the veteran radio comic, performs currently on television as well. Over the years he has been very closely associated with Lucky Strike.

But Your Hit Parade, which presents each week's top tunes as gorgeous "production numbers," remains the program most closely identified with Lucky Strike.

This Hit Parade program was produced with an eye to color TV. The "bullseye box" from which Dorothy Collins sings commercials will appear much changed to viewers accustomed to black-and-white (below).

pre-war assortment of magazines by the dozen, formed the core of the new print schedule. Special attempts were made to reach special groups outside their audiences: radio messages and placards in Spanish for the Southwest's border folk, special ads for other groups.

Era of good feeling

Through all this ran the new "Be Happy – Go Lucky" motif, intended to replace the old triphammer blows with a pleasant feeling. Oddly enough, Hahn's early work for the Company had involved the defense of its advertising against the Federal Trade Commission. As late as 1951, Hahn announced that the use of "less nicotine" as an advertising theme for *Lucky Strike* had been prohibited although "This fact was established by laboratory reports of chemical analyses, including one by the chemist for the U. S. Food and Drug Administration. The Commission did not deny this fact in its findings but concluded on the basis of conflicting expert testimony that this fact was not significant." (Suppression of the advertising theme did not, however, change the Manufacturing Department's target for nicotine content, which is still controlled.)

But it was part of Hahn's job in the new postwar climate of business-under-Government to reconcile sales policy with government relations as well as public relations. His advertising, keynoted by Dorothy Collins' wholesome and happy-go-lucky smile, was based on good taste in more ways than one. Factory facts confirmed the continuing emphasis on carefully controlled production; "better taste" and "it's all a matter of taste" were the central appeals, springing from that emphasis; and Hahn's own good taste, his refusal to match the extravagant claims of rivals, made American Tobacco the bellwether of a general drift away from the themes of the old campaigners.

And the old campaigners themselves were going. Riggio, seriously ill, could not continue as board Chairman and retired in January of 1951. In May of the same year the old prewar *Lucky Strike* triumvirate of Hill, Neiley and Lipscomb lost its last

Emphasis on taste distinguishes recent advertising for Lucky Strike cigarettes (right). Testimonials are taken only from actual smokers of the brand.

IT'S ALL A MATTER OF <u>TASTE</u>

CORN SILK, CUBEBS and MY MOST CONSTANT COMPANION

by **H. ALLEN SMITH**

Author and Humorist

I have changed my brand of cigarettes twice. I started with fine Illinois corn silk wrapped in the most delicate newsprint. Before long I switched to cubebs. I went from cubebs straight to Lucky Strikes. It was so long ago that I can't remember the year. I do know that Luckies have been my constant companion longer than my wife, and we've been married 26 years.

Since that first day with Luckies, I have switched jobs, razors, dentists, automobiles, phone numbers, and my stance on the tee. My taste in books, ties, food, music and even friends has changed, yet my taste for Luckies has remained constant. To me, they just taste better.

It is foolish to say that a man who is dedicated to one brand of cigarettes never gives the other brands a chance. There are occasions when a Lucky smoker, for reasons of war, financial embarrassment, pure hunger or the requirements of etiquette, must smoke other cigarettes. I have smoked them all. But not for long. What I like best is what tastes best. You know what.

Lucky Strike Sums Up

To smokers everywhere, Luckies taste better . . . and two facts explain why. In the first place, L.S./M.F.T.—Lucky Strike means fine tobacco. Then, too, Luckies are made better to taste better —to draw freely and smoke evenly.

So, Be Happy—Go Lucky. Remember, Luckies are made by The American Tobacco Company, America's leading manufacturer of cigarettes.

LUCKIES TASTE BETTER CLEANER, FRESHER, SMOOTHER!

Good News for Filter Tip Smokers!

Presenting
Herbert Tareyton
with the New Selective* Filter
and famous Tareyton quality

for real filtration and smoking satisfaction

Here, at last, is everything you've been looking for in a filter cigarette—the real filtration you want, and the full, rich taste of fine tobacco that makes smoking so enjoyable.

Tareyton's new Selective* Filter has unusual powers of selectivity which hold back elements that can detract from the pleasure of smoking. At the same time, the smooth, easy-drawing Tareyton Filter permits the full-bodied flavor of Tareyton's quality tobacco to come through to you for your complete smoking enjoyment.

Look for the red, white and blue stripes on the package. They identify the best in filtered smoking—Filter Tip Herbert Tareyton, the cigarette with a time-honored reputation for quality tobacco and the only filter cigarette with a genuine cork tip.

NOW 2 WAYS

REGULAR or FILTER
Both King Size with Genuine Cork Tip

＊ PATENTS PENDING

An entirely new concept in cigarette filtration. A filter tip of purified cellulose, incorporating Activated Charcoal, a filtering substance world-famous as a purifying agent, notably for air, water and beverages.

A SUPERIOR FILTER AT A POPULAR FILTER PRICE

The Herbert Tareyton Selective Filter Tip was wholly new, but the cigarette itself kept to an old essential—fine tobacco.

Administrators include Alfred F. Bowden, assistant to three successive Presidents (left), Charles Ganshow, *long with the American Cigarette and Cigar Company (center). Thomas P. Connors is Director of Traffic.*

survivor as Jim Lipscomb died, to be succeeded by James F. Strickland as President of American Suppliers.

Matters of taste

During the next two years, the example set by *Pall Mall* and *Tareyton* revolutionized the cigarette industry. In 1953, standard-length cigarettes retained only 70% of the market; *Lucky Strike*, *Camel* and *Chesterfield* now had a 55% combined share and even the top five standards (with *Philip Morris* and *Old Gold* added) had only 67%. Still, the Company's all-around position was better than it had ever been. *Lucky Strike* had a firm grasp on second place, with *Pall Mall* threatening to take over the No. 3 spot and the cork-tipped *Tareyton* up to seventh place. Altogether American's three brands combined sold more cigarettes than the 1940 total of *Lucky Strike*, *Camel*, *Chesterfield* and *Philip Morris*.

Although cigarettes generally tapered off slightly from the record 435,000,000,000 of 1952, the prospects were far from cloudy. In its 1954 Outlook Issue, the U. S. Department of Agriculture pointed out that "the number in the age brackets that compose the cigarette market is . . . increasing at an average of about 12 per cent per year." In this smoking-age group, President Hahn told a special meeting of stockholders, there were 113,000,000 per-

sons. And, the study estimated, "on the basis of population projections for 1960, there should be roughly 125,000,000 potential smokers by then."

Would their taste be significantly different from 1953 preferences? The filter-tipped cigarette seemed on the wax, its sales jumping from 1% of the total in 1952 to 3% the following year. Snorted a veteran tobaccoman, one of the Company's chief rivals: "Some folks will spoil good Bourbon with water, and some folks want filters." If the popular taste was there, American Tobacco would satisfy it. But Hahn and his 19,000 associates were particular about how they would satisfy it. The public demand, said the President, would have to be large enough to justify a venture into the new market; even more important, American's filter-tip would have to do an efficient job of filtration and not only that, but would have to do it without impairing the taste or flavor of the tobacco. These conditions amounted to a large order, and the Company refused, as always, to hurry its preparations at the expense of the final result. (In other departments, hurry was no worry: before commercial production of color television sets was under way, *Pall Mall* had a full commercial filmed in color —among the first of any national brand in any industry.)

When the new brand broke, in August of 1954, it was really something new. As the announcement

Reward Yourself
with the pleasure of smooth smoking

Smoke <u>longer</u> and <u>finer</u> and <u>milder</u> PALL MALL

Lighting up a PALL MALL just naturally goes with that feeling of satisfaction you get from a job well done. For PALL MALL pays you a rich reward in smoking pleasure—an extra measure of cigarette goodness.

Longer, yes – but greater length is only half the story

PALL MALLS are made longer—to travel the smoke further—to make it cooler and sweeter for you.

But you get more than greater length. Fine tobacco is its own best filter. And PALL MALL's richly-flavorful tobaccos are the finest quality money can buy. That's why PALL MALL gives you a smoothness, mildness, and satisfaction no other cigarette—*long or short*—can offer you.

THE FINEST QUALITY MONEY CAN BUY.

Your appreciation of PALL MALL quality has made in America's most successful and most imitated cigarette.

PALL MALL
FAMOUS CIGARETTES

·IN HOC SIGNO VINCES·

"WHEREVER PARTICULAR PEOPLE CONGREGATE"

Outstanding *and they are <u>mild!</u>*

Pall Mall red, a bright scarlet which distinguishes all its promotion, is fastidiously reproduced in the brand's advertising. To do this, Pall Mall uses two-color magazine art instead of the usual four-color.

With full color television in the offing, Pall Mall in 1953 turned out one of the first commercials on color film. As this is written, color TV technique does not permit the faithful transmission of filmed action in color. A black version of the commercial, however, appeared regularly on network TV in 1953.

explained, the Filter Tip *Herbert Tareyton* introduced a new concept in cigarette filtration. Mechanical filters hitherto on the market removed some of the solid or liquid particles from the cigarette smoke, but no significant proportion of the invisible gaseous elements.

Tareyton's Selective Filter Tip used purified cellulose to reduce passage of smoke solids to a predetermined level, without interfering with the passage of essential tobacco flavor. But in addition the tip contained a filtering substance to adsorb the gaseous constituents. The substance—activated charcoal—has long been used throughout the world to purify water, air, sugar, beverages and pharmaceuticals, is now considered the foremost purifier.

The Filter Tip *Tareyton* was perhaps the most dramatic single achievement in the Company's 25-year research on the composition of tobacco smoke.

Before American Tobacco's announcement of August 2, the public had scarcely realized that there were two broad classifications of compounds in cigarette smoke: the smoke solids—25,000,000,000 particles in a single puff—containing taste and flavor elements, including nicotine and the mixture often inaccurately called "tars"; and the invisible gases containing little or none of the taste and flavor elements. The "preferential removal" of the invisible gases was the unique, if not the only, feature of the new product.

The filter *per se* did not change the basic leaf requirements; if anything, quality became doubly important. As the press release noted, "The tobacco in filtered cigarettes must be specially chosen for quality, flavor and aroma; otherwise the smoke, after filtration, will be deficient in taste."

At the close of 1953, the corporate structure

was simplified by merging Hahn's old subsidiary, American Cigarette and Cigar, with the parent Company. Shortly afterward the cigar end of the business was streamlined by Charles Ganshow, as the old Henry Clay and Bock & Co., Ltd. was merged into Cuban Tobacco, along with The Havana Cigar and Tobacco Factories, Ltd. Saleswise, too, the cigar line was being streamlined. A. Gordon Findlay, who supervised clear Havana sales for American Cigarette and Cigar, took charge of all cigar sales for American Tobacco. The year before the Domestic Cigar Sales Department had started an extra Eastern push for *Roi-Tan*, already the nation's No. 1 10c cigar: and *Chancellor*, in a new green box, began to appear in test markets.

Publication of the 1953 annual report on March 1, 1954 proved the wisdom of being particular. The Company's increase in net income from operations—$5,368,000 over 1952—was greater than the combined increases registered by the three rivals which had been spun off from the combination forty-two years before. The Korean War price ceiling had been lifted in February of 1953, and American Tobacco's price increases had been characteristically modest. *Lucky Strike* was up-priced by 38c to $7.94 per thousand, as were all standard-length cigarettes; but *Pall Mall* and *Tareyton* were priced only slightly higher at $8.03 per thousand to jobbers, while most of their king-size rivals were lifted to $8.25. Adherence to the old formula—high quality plus low prices

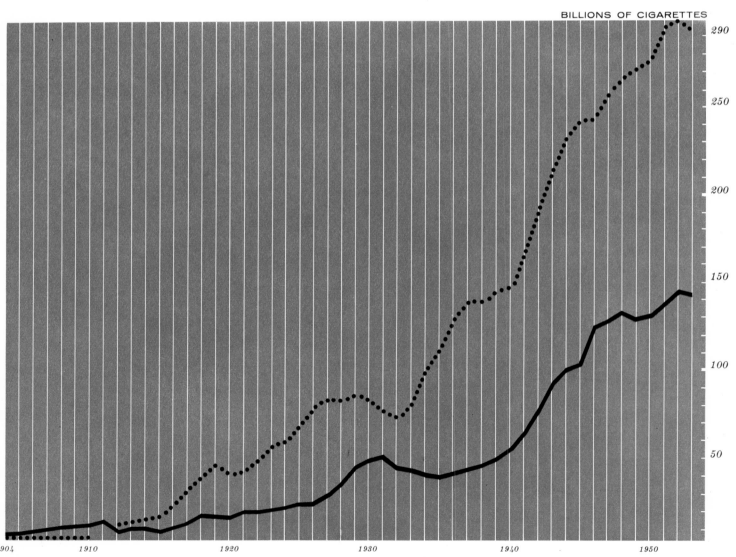

BILLIONS OF CIGARETTES

Rise of the Company's king-sized brands, Pall Mall and Herbert Tareyton, increased its share of total cigarette production from 23.5% in 1939 to nearly 32% in 1953. Increasing cigarette use is traced by sales of American Tobacco units (solid line) and production by the rest of the industry (dotted line).

For half a century, from James Duke to Paul Hahn, American Tobacco's New York offices have been in the Constable Building, 111 Fifth Avenue. The old address has even named a brand—"111" cigarettes.

Early in the second half-century, headquarters will move into this new skyscraper at Lexington Avenue and 42nd Street. On each of the seven floors to be occupied there will be room for an expansion of 25%.

to give maximum volume—would have gladdened the heart of Buck Duke himself.

Things were looking up, too, on the legislative front. True, excise taxes on cigarettes did not share in the reductions of April 1, 1954; at 8c per pack, they represented $4.00 of the $7.94 price to jobbers. But the U. S. Treasury encouraged hopes for an end to the prepayment system under which tax stamps had to be paid in advance. Financing these stamps involved tying up $60 million in cash throughout the year. Under the postpayment procedure used in virtually all other industries, the Company would save the interest cost on tied-up funds, approximately $1.8 million a year. Enabling legislation was passed in 1954, permitting weekly or monthly postpayment to begin the year following.

Before the first half-century was finished,

Hahn had arranged another departure for American Tobacco. A leasing agreement was signed for seven floors in New York's newest skyscraper, to rise at Lexington Avenue and 42nd Street. Sometime in 1955 or 1956, the old 111 Fifth Avenue address, once the city's finest, would be left behind. When J. B. Duke left his office in the building, the Company had sold 102,000,000,000 cigarettes. Seventy years after the first Bonsacks were installed in the Durham factory of W. Duke Sons & Company, the total had passed 2,300,000,000,000. What figure would the second half-century of American Tobacco bring?

One clause in the new headquarters lease revealed Paul Hahn's expectations. The American Tobacco Company was to occupy more space than it needed on each floor—enough for a 25% expansion in every department.

PICTURE CREDITS